OECD

MONETARY STUDIES SERIES

MONETARY POLICY
IN
ITALY

MAY 1973

The Organisation for Economic Co-operation and Development (OECD) was set up under a Convention signed in Paris on 14th December, 1960, which provides that the OECD shall promote policies designed :

— *to achieve the highest sustainable economic growth and employment and a rising standard of living in Member countries, while maintaining financial stability, and thus to contribute to the development of the world economy;*

— *to contribute to sound economic expansion in Member as well as non-member countries in the process of economic development;*

— *to contribute to the expansion of world trade on a multilateral, non-discriminatory basis in accordance with international obligations.*

The Members of OECD are Australia, Austria, Belgium, Canada, Denmark, Finland, France, the Federal Republic of Germany, Greece, Iceland, Ireland, Italy, Japan, Luxembourg, the Netherlands, Norway, Portugal, Spain, Sweden, Switzerland, Turkey, the United Kingdom and the United States.

CONTENTS

*
* *

5

*
**

LIST OF TABLES AND CHARTS

FOREWORD

This report forms part of a series of special studies on monetary policy undertaken by the Secretariat of the OECD at the request of the Economic Policy Committee. Each country has increasingly to formulate its own monetary policies within an international context. The purpose of these studies is to provide a better framework for the analysis of national monetary policies, and for international consultation regarding the use of monetary policy in Member countries for domestic demand management and balance of payments adjustment.

The need for detailed analysis on the working of monetary policy in different countries has been felt for various reasons:

i) In the recent period increased use has been made of monetary policy, and in more countries than previously, as a means of controlling demand, and as a consequence more evidence is becoming available as to the nature of its impact. It is useful to examine this evidence on an international basis and to compare the effects on demand of monetary policy in different countries.

ii) The volatility of international capital movements has increased. Though the scale of the effects to be attributed to monetary policy is difficult to quantify, the question is clearly of considerable importance for monetary authorities. Since the effects depend on the relative posture of monetary policies in different countries, they can clearly best be evaluated in the context of studies which examine the joint effects of different national monetary policies in at least the major financial countries.

The internal effects of monetary policy depend greatly on the economic and financial structure of the economy including the size of the public debt, the role of banks as financial intermediaries in the saving/investment process, the way in which housing is financed, and the scale and nature of consumer credit. These factors differ much from country to country. The external effects of monetary policy also depend to some extent on general institutional factors peculiar to different countries, and, in some cases, on the use made of policy instruments particularly designed to have external effects.

A series of country studies has, therefore, been envisaged which assembles the evidence about the working of monetary policy, taking into account differences in the economic and financial structure and the ways in which they have affected the choice of monetary instruments and the transmission process through which monetary policy has affected the financial and real sectors of the economy.

It has been decided to confine these studies, at least initially, to five or six countries whose monetary policies have been most important in influencing international capital movements. This report on Italy follows the study on monetary policy in Japan published in December 1972. Subsequent reports will be concerned with monetary policy in France, Germany, the United States, and possibly the United Kingdom. The results of these studies will later be integrated in a general report synthesizing the separate country studies.

The present study was prepared by the Monetary Division of the Department of Economics and Statistics, with valuable assistance from other members of the Department and from the staff of the Financial Directorate. It was discussed at meetings of official experts from the Member countries to be covered by the studies. The report is, however, published on my sole responsibility.

Emile van LENNEP
Secretary-General

I

INTRODUCTION

This study is divided into five parts. The present introductory section reviews the role of, and the limitations imposed upon, monetary policy in Italy in the light of that country's general economic background, fiscal policy and financial structure. Part II reviews briefly the basic instruments of monetary policy available to the monetary authorities, reserving a detailed description of the instruments to Appendix A and a chronology of their use to Appendix B, and it explains the framework of financial analysis employed by the Bank of Italy which relies mainly on the concept of the monetary base. Part III is a review of policy developments in their cyclical context and attempts to assess, by means of econometric and other evidence available, the impact of policy changes on financial variables. Part IV carries this evaluation further to the impact on major components of private expenditures. A concluding section attempts an overall assessment of the impact of policy.

a) GENERAL ECONOMIC BACKGROUND

Between 1960 and 1969 Italy experienced relatively rapid and stable growth, real output increasing at an average annual rate of close to 6 per cent. Nevertheless, there was almost throughout the period considerable unused resources. Full employment was approached only in 1962-63 and there was sizeable excess capacity in industry in the second half of the decade. The rate of change of prices was moderate by European standards except for a brief spurt in 1962-63 and again in 1968-69. The current account of the balance of payments was in surplus every year except 1963, and the surplus became both large and stable from 1965. Its effects on Italy's international reserves were largely offset by outflows of capital. The parity of the Italian lira remained unchanged and was at no time during this period subject to prolonged speculative attack.

Since the second half of 1969 the Italian economy has been in a state generally recognized to be highly unsatisfactory. Strikes and widespread social unrest in the course of that year led to sharp increases in wages and prices. Apart from a brief recovery early in 1970 the economy has never regained the momentum of earlier years. The gap between actual and potential output has widened considerably, particularly in 1971 when the growth rate was less than a third of the average for the 1960s. The current account surplus as well as the capital outflow have continued into this recent phase.

These broad generalizations about the Italian economy during the twelve years under study included the contribution made by economic policy towards

9

achieving the overall targets of faster economic growth, a high degree of price stability and external equilibrium. A major responsibility for shorter-run demand management was left to the monetary authorities, notably the Bank of Italy. Monetary policy was tightened vigorously in 1963 in the face of the worsening of the balance of payments and the acceleration of prices, and again in 1969. It is a major purpose of this study to review these two reversals of the generally expansionary policies pursued, to describe how policy instruments were changed and, insofar as this is possible, to assess the effects of monetary restraint on financial markets and real demand. Attention will also be given to the longer expansionary phases of policy. The main interest in this analysis of policy lies in the trans-mission mechanism (including the time lags) by which policy instruments make their influence felt on private investment— the most unstable of the demand components— private consumption and the capital account of the balance of payments.

One further general characteristic of the Italian economy must be kept in mind. A very difficult problem facing the Italian authorities is the *regional imbalance* in the form of a strong development differential between the North and the South. The latter is a predominantly agricultural region with per capita incomes only about half of those in the north-western, highly industrialised part of the country and considerable open and disguised unem-ployment. The acceleration of the economic development of the South has been one of the principal longer-term objectives of Italian economic policy and accordingly of monetary policy. While no attempt seems to have been made to prevent restrictive counter-cyclical policies in 1963-64 from affecting the South, an effort was made during the subsequent reflationary period, especially in 1968, to favour that region. The existence of regional differences complicates the problem of demand management in general, and the conduct of monetary policy in particular. There may be times when the developed region is in a situation of over-full employment while the under-developed region still has large reserves of idle manpower. Under such circumstances a generally restrictive monetary policy is not likely to be acceptable as the main answer to the problem of inflation because such a policy may aggravate the difficulties of the less favoured regions.

b) FISCAL POLICY

Fiscal policy has not made any major counter-cyclical contribution to demand management. The study of fiscal policy in seven OECD countries prepared by Bent Hansen[1] concluded that fiscal policy was only rarely ope-rating in a counter-cyclical way in the period 1955-65; supplementary calcu-lations based on the Hansen model carried out at the Bank of Italy and elsewhere reach similar conclusions for subsequent years. While shifts in fiscal policy have been larger after 1965 than before, they have rarely been well coordinated with the requirements of short-run demand management. A notable example is the shift from an expansionary to a contractionary stance of policy between 1966 and 1967; and in early 1970 there was an upsurge in public expenditures just at the time when private demand was

---

1. Bent Hansen, *Fiscal Policy in Seven Countries 1955-65*, OECD 1969, pp. 316-18.

picking up strongly. Since 1968 fiscal policy has generally been expansionary, though less so than intended.

There are two main reasons why it has been difficult to employ fiscal policy as an active instrument of demand management in Italy. One stems from the political difficulties common to all countries of securing appropriate and timely legislative action in the fiscal field. The other one stems from the difficulty of accelerating government expenditures for counter-cyclical purposes. Because of administrative rigidities rooted in the large size and uncoordinated nature of the governmental administrative apparatus, large unspent appropriations are carried over from year to year up to five years, giving rise to the so-called residual budgets (conti residui). For example, at the end of 1968 cumulative unspent appropriations of 5,800 billion lire were equal to 42 per cent of new expenditure authorised for 1969; and annual variations in this amount are quite substantial. Another factor posing difficulties for an anticyclical fiscal policy is the tradition of prefinancing increases in expenditures, i.e. of submitting a financing plan at the same time as the request for appropriations; typically the raising of funds through additional revenues or the issue of bonds has preceded the expenditures thereby making fiscal policy procyclical. Generally these uncertainties surrounding the evolution of the public finances have made it difficult for the monetary authorities to decide on an appropriate stance of monetary policy and to plan the scope of their own actions.

Fiscal policy has not been seriously constrained by considerations of debt management. The demand for long-term bonds from both the commercial banks and the non-bank public has been substantial, and the Postal System has been a steady, though on the average relatively modest, source of finance. In recent years when these sources have become increasingly inadequate, central bank credit has been available; the Bank of Italy is required by law to grant the Treasury unsecured overdraft facilities of up to 14 per cent of current ordinary appropriations. This level has been approached in recent years, but as there is no limit to the Bank's ability to buy Treasury bills or Government long-term securities either directly from the Treasury or in the open market, this has not hindered the growth of expenditures in recent years when the Bank of Italy has become the main source of finance. On the other hand the growth and seasonal volatility of the Treasury's borrowing requirements have at times complicated the tasks of monetary management (see page 22 below), though the desirability of a rapid growth in liquidity to boost a sluggish economy and the possibilities for offsetting the shifting liquidity effects of Government operations have generally facilitated the resolving of such complications (see Appendix A, IV).

c) FINANCING BY SECTOR

The Italian financial system has been evolving considerably over the period under study. Figures for a single year, or even a short span of years, cannot, therefore, give an adequate picture of the financial structure for the period as a whole.[1] The tables in the present and the following section refer to averages for the three-year period 1966-68 which is the most recent phase of steady growth and expansionary monetary policies, but occasional com-

---

1. A more detailed analysis of the Italian financial system and its evolution will be found in *The Capital Market, International Capital Movements, Restrictions on Capital Operations in Italy*, OECD Committee for Invisible Transactions (forthcoming).

11

ments will be made about subsequent shifts. Tables A1-5 in the Data Annex give annual figures for the whole period under study.

An important feature of the Italian financial structure is the relatively large financial deficit of the *public sector* (Table 1). In the years 1966-68, its deficit was 2.4 per cent to GNP and it has been growing in recent years. The central government's gross savings are not usually large enough to cover the sizeable volume of capital expenditures including transfers to the local authorities. Besides, the social security system has constantly shown a net financial deficit. The central government relies largely on the short-term credit of the Bank of Italy, and the issuance of government bonds to finance its financial deficit. The local authorities have also recorded a net financial deficit for a number of years. Banks and special credit institutions as well as the central administration have been the major sources of their external funds.

The enterprise sector— including housing and publicly owned enter-prises such as ENEL, ENI, IRI, etc.— has also shown a large financial deficit, amounting to 5.5 per cent of GNP in the years 1966-68. While internal funds have been steadily rising throughout the 1960s, companies have relied increasingly on external funds to finance real investment and the accumulation of financial assets (which has largely taken the form of deposits with the banks, other types of financial investments remaining unim-portant throughout the 1960s). The enterprise sector raises its external funds mainly in the form of borrowing from banks, special credit institutions, and other financial intermediaries: during the years 1966-69, such borrowing amounted to almost 80 per cent of external funds (which in turn was equal to 50 per cent of its real investment). Private companies have not relied much on the issue of securities (see pp. 16-18); accordingly the direct contri-bution of the household sector to the financing of enterprises through the securities market is almost negligible in Italy. Typically, about half of the financing of investment in housing has been financed directly by individuals: a small and declining share has come from public funds and the remainder from financial institutions, about evenly divided between specialised credit institutions and others.

The household sector placed a large part of their savings in deposits with the banking system. But the holding of demand deposits is of smaller relative importance than in most other industrial countries, reflecting the limited use of cheques by private individuals in Italy. In the last two or three years there has been a shift from savings to demand deposits, also on the parts of households, due to the higher rates paid on demand deposits by banks. In recent years, the household sector has also been an important supplier of funds to the securities market.

d) FINANCIAL INTERMEDIARIES AND MARKETS

Tables 2 and 3, supplemented by Table A4 of the Data Annex, provide an illustration of the flow of funds through the main Italian financial insti-tutions. The banking system proper hereinafter referred to as "banks"[1] is

---

1. The banking system consists of commercial banks, savings banks, and their central institutions. It is worth noting that Italian savings banks have gradually come to handle practically the same credit operations as the commercial banks and, very often, operate in direct competition with them. As for the differences in the regula-tions affecting the banks' compulsory reserve requirements, see Appendix A.

	House-holds	Enter-prises[1]	Public Adminis-tration	Total Domestic Sectors
1. Gross Savings[2]	11.0	11.7	—	22.7
2. Gross Investment	—	17.2	2.4	19.6
3. Net Financial Position (1—2)	11.0	−5.5	−2.4	3.1

FINANCING BY SECTOR
PER CENT OF TOTAL

	Households	Enterprises and Housing	Public Administration
1. Gross Savings	91.4	57.4	−0.1
2. External Funds	8.6	42.6	100.1
3. Total Sources of Funds (1 + 2)	100.0	100.0	100.0
4. Financial Assets	100.0	21.7	48.1
5. Investment	—	78.3	51.9
6. Total Uses of Funds (4 + 5)	100.0	100.0	100.0

1. Including housing.
2. Including net capital transfers,
Source: Tables A1—A3 of Data Annex.

by far the most important intermediary, collecting almost two-thirds of all funds channelled through financial institutions and supplying almost half of total credit to non-financial sectors of the economy.   The banks are also an important source of funds for the specialised credit institutions, the lending by which accounts for an additional 20 per cent.   Insurance companies are of very minor importance.   The Cassa Depositi e Prestiti (Central Post Office Savings Fund) purveys a sizeable portion of total credit raised by the public sector (excluding publicly-owned enterprises).   The foreign contribution was negligible in the period 1966 to 1968, but it increased to about 23 per cent in 1969-70, when, as a result of the difficult conditions of the domestic bond market, the special credit institutions and some of the large state-owned corporations stepped up their recourse to the Euromarkets. There follows a brief description of the main financial institutions and markets in Italy.

Banks (*Aziende di Credito*)

Banks, of which there are over 1,200 in Italy operating some 10,000 branches, collect funds through demand (chequeing) accounts and time deposits up to 18 months' maturity.   They are thus indirectly constrained

13

TABLE 2. SOURCES OF FUNDS BORROWED BY NON-FINANCIAL SECTORS
PER CENT OF TOTAL, 1966-68 AVERAGE

Lenders \ Borrowers	House-hold	Enter-prise	Govern-ment[1]	Total
Financial Intermediaries:				
1. Bank of Italy	—	—	2	1
2. Banks	47	50	42	47
3. Special Credit Institutions	49	27	8	22
4. Insurance Companies	1	1	1	1
5. Cassa Depositi e Prestiti	—	2	15	6
6. Total (1 + 2 + 3 + 4)	97	80	68	77
Non-financial Domestic:				
7. Household	—	6	31	2
8. Enterprise	—	3	—	2
9. Government[1]	3	6	-4	15
10. Total (7 + 8 + 9)	3	15	27	19
11. *Foreign*	—	5	1	3
12. *Non-identified Borrowing*	—	—	4	1
13. Total (6 + 10 + 11 + 12)	100	100	100	100
Memorandum Item:				
Sector's borrowing as percentage of total	7	57	36	100

1. General government, excluding the Cassa Depositi e Prestiti.
Source: Bank of Italy, *Annual Reports.*

in the maturities of the credit they extend, although they can and do make intermediate (18 to 60 months) and long-term credits up to a certain pre-fixed percentage of their deposits. Moreover, owing to the widespread use of almost automatic renewals, a certain amount of formally short-term loans are, in practice, of a longer-term nature. Banks are also permitted to own stock in, or even to control entirely, "special credit institutions", whose activities are described below. The nine largest banks (accounting for about 45 per cent of banking activity) and about 90 other banks (accounting for another 20 per cent of banking activity) are either owned by the state directly, or through IRI,[1] or, in the case of savings banks, organised as foundations. However, the management of publicly-owned banks does not seem to have differed substantially from that of private banks, and, in any case, the monetary authorities' controls have been applied uniformly to both categories of banks. In recent years, the major banks have considerably expanded their international business by participating extensively in the activities of the Eurodollar and Eurobond markets, by taking an active part in the setting-up of international consortia, and by increasing their participations in international ventures.

1. Istituto per la Ricostruzione Industriale: the major holding company for publicly-owned enterprises. It controls a large variety of industrial and service enterprises, including, among others, shipyards, steel mills, and airlines.

14

Table 3. RESOURCES OF FINANCIAL INSTITUTIONS
Per cent of total, 1966-68 average

Lenders / Borrowers	Bank of Italy	Banks	Special credit institutions	Insurance companies	Cassa Depositi e Prestiti	Total
Domestic non-financial sectors:						
1. Households	42	38	47	80	79	44
2. Enterprises........................	5	30	1	15	24	21
3. Government	—	2	12	—	–23	3
i) Central government	(—)	(—)	(12)	(—)	(—)	(3)
ii) Other	(—)	(2)	(—)	(—)	(–23)	(—)
4. Total (1 + 2 + 3)	47	70	60	95	80	68
5. *Foreign*	–1	8	—	—	—	4
6. *Total non-financial (4 + 5)*	46	78	60	95	80	72
Financial intermediaries:						
7. Bank of Italy.....................	—	10	—	—	14	7
8. Banks	40	9	39	—	—	17
9. Special credit institutions	7	1	—	1	—	1
10. Insurance companies	—	—	2	1	—	1
11. Cassa Depositi e Prestiti	—	—	–1	—	—	—
12. Total (7 to 11)	47	20	40	2	14	26
13. *Non-identified flows*	7	2	—	3	6	2
14. Total resources (6 + 12 + 13)	100	100	100	100	100	100
Memorandum item:						
Resources of the institutions as a percentage of total resources of financial institutions	9	63	20	3	5	100

Source: Bank of Italy, *Annual Reports.*

Special credit institutions (Istituti Speciali di Credito)

These institutions operate typically in the area of medium and long-term credit. They raise funds mainly through long-term bond issues in the domestic and international capital markets, but also, to a limited extent, through time deposits and debentures of 18 to 60 months' maturity. Almost half of their lending is to the enterprise sector, including public utilities, and an additional 30 per cent is channelled to the housing sector. One group of institutions extends credit, including in this case short-term credit, to agriculture. A large and increasing part of the lending of special credit institutions takes place at subsidized interest rates for socially desirable projects in the less developed areas of Italy, notably the South, and for facilitating the longer-term financing of small and medium-sized enterprises. Generally the volume and terms of subsidized credit have not been varied to serve purposes of short-run demand management. Part of the cost of the subsidy is borne by the Treasury.

The most important institutions are public or quasi-public in nature.[1] Depository banks have largely contributed to the setting-up of the special credit institutions by establishing "special sections" authorised to extend medium-term credit to specified economic sectors. The flow of funds from depository banks to the special credit institutions is also very important, accounting for almost 40 per cent of the increase in the institutions' liabilities. These funds are usually channelled to the special institutions through the opening of overdraft facilities, and through the placing of the institutions' long-term securities with the banks and their central organisations. There is a network of industrial credit institutions operating on a regional level with the assistance of a special refinancing institution, *Mediocredito Centrale*. On the whole, the importance of the specialised institutions has been growing relatively to that of banks throughout the period under study: the average annual rate of growth of their lending has been 17 per cent in the decade as against 13 per cent for the banks. Subsidized credit to the enterprise sector, which at the beginning of the 1960s constituted little more than one third of total enterprise indebtedness, has risen to about three fourths a decade later.

Other financial intermediaries

There are more than 170 private insurance companies and one public company in Italy, but their direct lending and investment activities are largely prescribed and practically insignificant. There are also certain government agencies, notably the Central Post Office Savings Fund (Cassa Depositi e Prestiti) which functions as a special department of the Treasury. The Cassa collects funds through ordinary savings book deposits, and postal savings certificates, but also accepts current account deposits from enterprises and public organisations. The funds collected are utilised for extending medium and long-term credits to local authorities and, to a lesser extent, to public autonomous agencies and enterprises. Social security institutions, whose activities are decentralised, use their reserve funds for investment in securities and the extension of credit to local authorities. Their importance as suppliers of funds to the economy is, however, very limited indeed. At present, there is no domestic fund of the open-end type,[2] but a few foreign funds have been authorised to operate in Italy.

Security markets

The Italian issue market for *bonds* is one of the largest in the OECD area: in 1965 to 1971, the ratio of net issues to GNP averaged 7 per cent, a very high percentage by international standards. On the supply side, a striking feature is the clear, indeed nearly complete, predominance of the government, state-owned enterprises and the specialised credit institutions and the corresponding, almost negligible, importance of net issues by private enterprises: in fact, since 1967, redemptions have largely offset

---

1. The largest of these institutions is Istituto Mobiliare Italiano (IMI), which makes loans of 5 to 20 years' duration, usually secured by mortgages.
2. A bill regulating the setting-up and organisation of domestic open-end funds was submitted to the Italian Parliament in 1969, but it has not yet received approval. The bill prescribes that at least half the funds of such institutions be invested in Italian securities.

16

TABLE 4. SUPPLY AND DEMAND ON THE ITALIAN BOND MARKET
Per cent of total, 1966-1968 average

Lenders / Borrowers	Govern-ment	Public enter-prises[1]	Private enter-prises	Special credit insti-tutions	Foreign	Total
1. Central Bank	17	2	—	—	20	7
2. Banks	48	50	32	44	29	46
3. Insurance companies and special credit institutions	4	6	3	4	−2	4
4. Cassa Depositi e Prestiti[2]	−1	−3	—	−1	—	−1
5. Companies						
6. Households	32	45	65	53	53	44
7. Rest of the world						
8. Total	100	100	100	100	100	100

1. National Electric Energy Agency (ENEL); National Institute for Hydro-carbon (ENI); Institute for Industrial Reconstruction (IRI); Autonomous Public Agency for National Railways (FFSS).
2. Including purchases by pension funds.
Source: OECD *Financial Statistics* and Table A5 of Data Annex.

TABLE 5. THE ISSUE MARKET FOR SHARES
Per cent of total, 1966-68 Average

ISSUERS

1. Public enterprises	16
2. Private enterprises	70
3. Financial institutions	14
4. Total net issues (1 + 2 + 3)	100

HOLDERS

5. Banks	—
6. Insurance companies	4
7. Companies	47
8. Households	11
9. Rest of the world	37
10. Other	1
11. Total (5 to 10)	100

Source: OECD *Financial Statistics.*

gross issues (Table A5 of the Data Annex). The reluctance of Italian companies to enter into the market has been mainly due to fiscal reasons: as taxes on new issues have accounted for almost one-third of the coupon rate, private enterprises have found it more advantageous to satisfy their long-term financial needs by borrowings from the special credit institutions.[1] To finance their growing lending activities, these institutions have substan-

1. This tax will be modified with effect from 1974, without, however, fully removing the incentive to finance via the special credit institutions (or the banks) rather than through bond issues.

tially increased their recourse to the bond market, to which they have access at favourable conditions, thus becoming the largest borrower thereon. The government's share in total net issues has ranged from between 35 and 40 per cent and that of public enterprises never deviated much from 20 per cent. The capital supply structure of the Italian bond market is characterised by the fundamental role played by the banking system: depository banks absorb between one-third and one-half of total issues, to which a substantial contribution by the Bank of Italy— usually limited to government bonds— has to be added (Table 4). On the other hand, institutional investors and the other financial institutions take up only a negligible share of total net issues. The supply of funds from the private non-financial sector, mainly households, was of particular importance during the period 1966 to 1968, as a result of the Central Bank's policy of stabilisation of bond prices. In 1969-71 the share of purchases by the non-financial public declined somewhat below the range of 40 to 50 per cent reached during the earlier period.

Towards the end of the 1960s, net issues of *shares* accelerated markedly (Table A5). Over the period 1965 to 1971, the ratio of new issues to GNP averaged 1.3 per cent, a percentage slightly higher than that prevailing in most OECD countries, and it reached the very high value of 2 per cent in 1970. Well over two-thirds of new shares are issued by private non-financial enterprises, while issues by public enterprises account for an additional 15 per cent (Table 5). No substantial shift in the composition of the supply of funds to the market has been recorded over the recent period. Financial institutions play a very modest role, and the purchases by households remain relatively small. On the other hand, intercompany holdings appear to be very important since almost 50 per cent of new funds flowing to the market come from the enterprise sector. Finally a very large proportion of new issues is taken up by non-residents. In this respect, it must, however, be noted that data on foreign purchases of Italian securities are likely to be affected by the volume of illegal export of banknotes. In fact, part of this exported capital is probably repatriated in Italy and reinvested under the cover of a foreign name.

While the markets for long-term finance are well developed, an active *money market* in the sense in which this term is used in the United States or the United Kingdom does not exist. Surplus short-term funds in a commercial bank or specialised credit institution are either invested in deposits with one of the larger banks or a central credit institution, in Treasury bills or in foreign money markets, provided that the latter possibility has not been blocked by the regulations of the Bank of Italy (page 24). Interest rates in the interbank deposit market were subject to a legal maximum between 1962 and 1969; the Treasury bill rate was completely stabilised until May 1969, as the Bank of Italy stood ready to issue bills on tap and repurchase them at a steady rate. The rigidity of these rates and of the discount rate prevented the growth of the domestic money market and its widening to attract non-bank funds. The attitude of the authorities was modified from 1969: the maximum on interbank deposit rate was removed; the rate on "free" Treasury bills (i.e. those held by banks in excess of compulsory requirements) was allowed to rise; the discount rate was raised. But conjunctural difficulties have so far prevented any important development of the money market.

18

Practically all credit in the Italian economy flows through channels potentially amenable to the direct influence of the public authorities in general, and the monetary authorities in particular. All "banks" are subject to minimum reserve requirements on deposits and to most of the other monetary policy instruments described elsewhere in this paper. The special credit institutions are also subject to specific controls over their fund-raising activities; in particular, all their security issues— with the exception of mortgage bonds (cartelle confiarie)[1] and of those debentures available on tap, such as savings certificates (buoni fruttiferi)— must obtain prior authorisation from the Interministerial Committee on Credit and Savings which acts on the basis of advice from the Bank of Italy. Issues of securities by private and public enterprises as well as by local authorities and public agencies require official permission; the need for prior authorisation applies to any issue of shares and to issues of bonds, the total amount of which exceeds 500 million lire. Borrowing from non-residents in the form of financial credits and loans, and through issue of securities on foreign capital markets, may also be affected by the authorities' comprehensive powers of supervision and control.[2]

1. It must, however, be noted that issues of mortgage bonds are limited by specific ceilings related to the size of the equity capital of the issuing institute.
2. Under the OECD Code of Liberalisation of Capital Movements, Italy has lodged full reservations in respect of these inward capital movements.

II

THE INSTRUMENTS AND THE ANALYTICAL
FRAMEWORK FOR MONETARY POLICY

The Italian monetary authorities possess a large range of instruments of monetary policy. From Part I it will be obvious that the scope for intervention in financial markets is considerable. An increasing share of total credit flows has been channelled through special institutions (page 15) whose lending operations are supervised and subsidised by the public authorities. Although this direct influence has not been used for the purposes of short-run demand management but rather to improve the geographical and/or sectoral allocation of resources, it has definite implications for the working of the more indirect of monetary policy effects based on classical instruments with which this study is primarily concerned. For example, the increasing share of subsidised loans in total credit flows has modified the impact of the upward shift in other interest rates charged of borrowers since 1969, though it is likely that some of this effect has been offset by additional increases in the cost of credit which does not qualify for subsidies. More relevant from a short-term viewpoint are the comprehensive powers of controlling access to the capital market (page 19), which have at times been used counter-cyclically, notably in 1969-70. Nevertheless, the control of new issues has mainly been exercised to improve the technical functioning of the bond market by assuring a growth of supply roughly matching the estimated demand. The present part, therefore, is confined to description of those instruments of monetary policy which have been designed to influence the availability and cost of credit supplied by the banking system. But the existence and practices of these institutions imply that the scope for influencing credit in Italy goes well beyond the range of these instruments.

a) THE INSTRUMENTS AND THEIR USE

In their attempt to assure desired developments in the cost, overall availability and composition (between direct lending and bond purchases) of bank credit and in long-term interest rates, the Bank of Italy has used four main instruments:

  i) sales and purchases of government securities and other debt management actions;

  ii) changes in the volume and— since 1969— the cost of its credit to the commercial banks;

21

iii) variations in reserve requirements, and

iv) changes in the regulations pertaining to the net foreign position of the commercial banks.

A detailed description of these instruments may be found in Appendix A[1] and a chronology of their use in Appendix B.

Purchases and sales of government or government-guaranteed securities were of limited importance until 1966, when, as a result of the more explicit policy of stabilising long-term rates, interventions in the open market to smooth fluctuations became more frequent. From the same year the Bank also began buying substantial amounts of government long-term bonds at issue to facilitate the financing of rapidly rising government deficits. This substantial involvement in the bond market has continued after the experiment with pegged bond rates ended in mid-1969; under the impact of continuing government deficits and mounting difficulties of selling the debt instruments to the public, these debt management operations have continued to be designed towards containing the tendency for interest rates to rise. Another factor pushing the Bank of Italy into lending to the government in the form of subscribing to bond issues is that the other form in which it may lend, viz, overdrafts on the Treasury's account, has been moving close to a statutory ceiling of 14 per cent of annual expenditures for the last three years.[2]

As the government's banker and financial adviser, the Bank of Italy is constantly faced with the problem of making the management of the public debt roughly consistent with the targets for liquidity creation. In practice, the problem is approached in the following way: the Treasury submits an advance estimate of the monthly borrowings requirements. In months were it is large and positive, the Bank of Italy reacts to the estimate by proposing a breakdown between the five main forms of financing:

i) sale of long-term securities to the public,

ii) absorption of Treasury bills in commercial bank compulsory reserves,

iii) sale of "free" Treasury bills,

iv) inflow of postal deposits, and

v) the residual finance to be forthcoming from the Bank itself either in the form of bond subscriptions or overdrafts, as the case may be.

Of these, *(ii)* is known at the beginning of each month because bank required reserves are calculated on the basis of deposit levels of the previous month. The other components are estimated from observed historical relationships and the assumptions made about interest rates on the three categories of financial assets: Government bonds, postal deposits and Treasury bills. The form of financing which reduce the liquidity impact of the deficit are *(i)* and *(iii)* and the estimate of— or rather the decision with respect to—

---

1. For an analysis of the use of the two latter instruments see also M. Fratianni, "Bank Credit and Money Supply Processes in an Open Economy: A Model Applicable to Italy", *Metroeconomica*, April 1972, pp. 24-69.

2. From the viewpoint of overall monetary management, it is of course unimportant whether central bank financing takes the form of bond purchases or direct lending. It may also be noted that even the effects on interest rates are similar, since the increase in the Bank of Italy's security portfolio normally takes the form of subscriptions to new issues rather than purchases in the open market.

these items is determined by the relative acceptability of higher interest rates and the liquidity creation which their avoidance would require.

The Bank of Italy supplies *credit to the commercial banks* in various forms, none of which is in principle automatic. In regulating the volume of credit to banks the Bank of Italy has been relying largely on quantitative rationing rather than on changes in the discount rate. The discount rate remained unchanged at 3.5 per cent unitil 1969, when it was raised to 4 per cent; subsequently it has been used more actively in the interval between 4 and 5.5 per cent.[1] There are two main forms of lending by the Bank of Italy to commercial banks:

  i) rediscounting of eligible paper, and
  ii) advances on collateral.

Of these two forms of lending, advances have generally been preferred; they have usually been granted within 3 to 5 per cent of the volume of deposits of the individual bank.[2] Since 1967 ordinary advances have been supplemented by additional fixed-term advances; from 1969 penalty rates have been changed on lending above a certain level. In the early part of the period commercial banks tended to observe a cartel agreement linking minimum lending rates to the discount rate, but in recent years the agreement has tended to become increasingly inoperative, thus weakening the impact of discount rate changes on actual bank lending rates. Since the beginning of 1971 an interbank agreement has been in effect which specifies maximum deposit rates. There remains some rigidity in Italian deposit and lending rates, but it seems likely that published statistics may overstate this phenomenon.

It would be difficult to say to what extent the use of central bank credit is influenced by moral suasion exercised by the Bank of Italy. The scope for use of this informal instrument is considerable, given the important role of the nine largest banks (page 14). It may be a helpful factor in this connection that bank loans above a certain size are subject to approval by the Bank of Italy. Though this power is meant as a device to protect depositors and has not been used deliberately as an anti-cyclical instrument to control aggregate demand for bank credit, it remains a possibility that, in times of credit stringency, an increase in the number of refusals of large loans could reinforce other measures of credit restraint.

Variations in reserve requirements against commercial bank deposits have only been used exceptionally. Requirements have been lowered across the board once, in 1962, but in 1965 the assets usable to meet them were extended by the inclusion of a wide range of long-term securities. This had the effect of virtually freeing increases in time and savings deposits from any requirement in the form of primary reserves. In late

---

1. Another, less important, reason why frequent changes in the discount rate were avoided has been explained by the Bank of Italy as follows (BIS, *Some Questions Relating to the Structure of Interest Rates,* July 1968, page 19): traditionally the Central bank pays interest on the reserve balances of the commercial banks. Therefore, any change in the discount rate would be, eventually, followed by a corresponding change in the interest paid on required reserves. But the time lag with which this took place, on the occasions when the discount rate was actually changed, was not negligible, and there is no legal constraint which prevents the Bank of Italy from varying the two rates independently. Actually in 1971 and 1972 the discount rate and the rate on advances were lowered without reducing the rate paid on compulsory reserves.

2. See Chart B of Appendix A.

1970, the Bank of Italy allowed the commercial banks to substitute certain long-term bonds for cash or Treasury bills. These modifications of reserve requirements have been made for structural purposes rather than for reasons of short-term monetary management. They form part of the long series of efforts undertaken by the Italian authorities to enlarge and improve the functioning of the bond market, including those parts of the market in which the bank itself is prevented from operating directly. From the viewpoint of monetary management, the net effect of the 1965 liberalisation has been to increase markedly the impact on bank loans of changes in bank liquidity (see page 45), thus giving the management of the latter much greater leverage. It may be argued, however, that since the volume of required reserves now depends crucially on the composition of deposits, the predictability of this leverage has diminished. The development of effective reserve requirement ratios, i.e. of reserves held in the form of cash (monetary base) is shown in Chart 1.

The management of the net position of the Italian commercial banks vis-à-vis non-residents (net foreign position) has been used actively on several occasions since 1960. The objective of applying this instrument has been both to protect Italy's official international reserves from the fluctuations in the current and non-monetary capital accounts and to influence domestic liquidity creation. Although it has proved useful on both fronts, it would be fair to note that the main aim of using it was external; on one important occasion (1962) a relaxation in the regulations pertained only to the net position in foreign currency while leaving the net position in domestic currency vis-à-vis non-residents unchanged. In any case, this instrument is not well designed for continuous short-run management of the base and it has not been used actively during the period 1968-71. The regulation has typically taken the form of setting a floor under the net foreign position of the commercial banks. When the regulation was first strongly relied upon in 1963, Italian commercial banks were heavily indebted to foreign correspondents and the floor set was therefore significantly negative. Subsequently, this floor was raised gradually to a requirement of a zero net foreign position. Towards the end of the period, when the problem shifted to the prevention of capital outflows from Italy, the regulation took the form of a ceiling on the net foreign asset position. The regulations, which have remained unchanged from mid-1969, preserve the freedom of banks to manage their gross positions in accordance with their preferences. The management of the net foreign position has been supplemented by indirect means through *swap* facilities at preferential rates for banks, during the process of complying with changes in the regulations. Throughout the period the Bank of Italy refrained from intervening on the normal forward market, which is in any case not used extensively in Italy.

Of the four main instruments, variations in reserve requirements is one major determinant of the demand by banks for reserves or, from a different perspective, the credit and deposit multipliers; the three others directly change the volume of liquid claims held by the Italian private sector— banks or others— on the monetary authorities or the rest of the world. Since the demand for such claims by the non-bank public may in the short-run be regarded as approximately unaffected by variations in the policy instruments (pp. 44-45), the immediate impact of such varia-

24

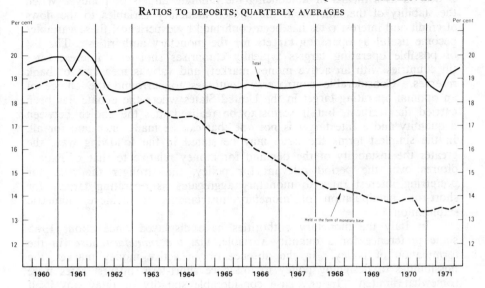

tions shows up mainly in a change in the reserve position of the banks; and this change in combination with existing reserve requirements will determine the ability of banks to meet the demand for credit. Compared to the use of policy instruments in other countries, it may be said in summary that changes in the security portfolio of the Bank of Italy— at least in the form of sales and purchases in the open market— and changes in reserve requirements have been used rather less for short-run purposes in Italy, although the former instrument has been acquiring importance since 1969; variations in central bank lending and in the regulations pertaining to the banks' net foreign position, on the other hand, have been used relatively more in the two phases where policy was used with the greatest vigour.[1] This choice of instruments as well as the way in which they have been used, notably the emphasis on rationing rather than cost as the main limitation on central bank credit, suggest that the Italian monetary authorities have been aiming at influencing initially the volume of bank credit rather than the level of interest rates. The following section reviews the framework for monetary analysis used by the Bank of Italy which broadly confirms this preliminary conclusion.

b) THE DESIGN OF MONETARY POLICY

The monetary authorities in most countries have chosen one or more monetary magnitudes on which they see themselves as operating in order to achieve the indirect control over the availability and cost of credit which

---

1. In these respects Italy bears some resemblance to Japan which has also relied rather heavily on these two instruments; see *Monetary Policy in Japan*, OECD 1972, pages 25-26 and 29.

is desired as a means of influencing the ultimate targets of policy. When the stability of the links from the chosen monetary variables to the flows of credit and interest rates has been confirmed by experience, these variables become useful as operating targets for the monetary authorities. The list of possible operating targets typically comprises shor-term interest rates (in countries with an active money market) and various measures of bank reserves. Considerable controversy continues to surround the choice of an optimal operating target in the United States where the debate has been carried the farthest, but it seems to be realised that the choice between a quantity and a rate target is not one that can be made once and for all. In the simplest terms the issue may be stated in the following way: the greater the instability of the demand for money relative to that of expenditures over the period relevant for policy, the stronger the case for preferring interest rates to monetary aggregates as operating targets for short-run manipulation of monetary instruments to achieve domestic stabilisation.

In Italy the monetary authorities have displayed since about 1965 some preference for a quantity variable, viz. *the monetary base,* in the formulation of policy. In the absence of an active money market, the possibilities of designing policy to influence short-term interest rates were somewhat limited. In any case considerable stability of rates was itself an aim of policy during the long period of expansion in 1964-69; it was only from April 1969 that the Treasury bill rate at the weekly auctions was allowed to move above the low level firmly maintained throughout the 1960s— around 3.6 per cent. Given the rigidity of short-term rates, the authorities have concentrated on a formulation of policy in terms of initially bank excess reserves and subsequently the broader concept of the monetary base, but with interest rates on long-term government bonds as an important supplementary target in one period.

It is possible to follow in the Annual Reports of the Bank of Italy the gradual substitution of the monetary base for excess reserves.[1] To discuss the relative merits of the two concepts it is necessary to look at the definition of the monetary base. Looked at from *the uses,* i.e. the form in which it is held, the base consists of liquid claims on the rest of the world, the government and the Bank of Italy held by the Italian private sector, banks and non-banks (Table 6). The non-banks— the public and the specialised financial institutions hold about two-thirds of the outstanding monetary base in the form of currency (notes and coin) and current and savings deposits with the postal system which are also included in the base as defined by the Italian authorities. The remainder consists of the reserves, required or excess, of the banks.[2] Table 6 shows the composition of changes in the uses in the most recent four years. The total stock

---

1. See Bank of Italy *Annual Reports* 1965 (p. 84), 1966 (p. 84), 1967 (p. 91) and 1968 (pp. 181-82); page numbers refer to the abridged English version of the publication. See also A. Fazio, "Monetary Base and the Control of Credit in Italy", *Banca Nazionale del Lavoro Quarterly Review,* June 1969.
2. Also included in the definition are bank assets which are readily convertible into base money, e.g. through rediscounting. The treatment of Treasury bills varies according to whether they are part of required reserves or excess reserves; since those bills forming part of the latter have not been redeemable on demand since May 1969, they are excluded from the base. A disaggregated quarterly series for the base has been published in the Bank of Italy *Bollettino,* January-February 1972.

TABLE 6. USES OF MONETARY BASE
BILLION OF LIRE

			Changes during				Levels out-standing on 31 dec. 1971
			1968	1969	1970	1971	
I.	HELD BY NON-BANKS		577	1,152	985	1,783	14,707
	A.	Non-bank public	519	1,095	769	1,825	14,244
		of which:					
		i) Notes and coin	207	707	505	667	7,139
		ii) Demand and savings deposits with Postal Administration	355	373	237	1,133	6,977
		iii) Deposits with Treasury and Bank of Italy, and, until May 1969, Treasury bills which could be redeemed on demand at no loss of interest	–43	15	27	25	128
	B.	Special credit institutions: Vault cash and deposits with Bank of Italy	58	57	216	–42	463
II.	HELD BY BANKS		664	93	1,169	1,529	8,550
	A.	Compulsory reserves against deposit liabilities and money orders outstanding[1]	403	416	782	1,162	6,700
		of which:					
		i) Cash deposits with Bank of Italy	274	346	529	730	4,018
		ii) Treasury bills	109	70	–17	380	2,277
		iii) Long-term bonds[1]	20	—	270	52	405
	B.	Excess reserves (liquid assets)	261	–323	387	367	1,850
		of which:					
		i) Vault cash	71	14	26	6	370
		ii) Free deposits with Bank of Italy	11	9	76	391	616
		iii) Undrawn portion of collateral loan line with Bank of Italy	8	–24	212	87	786
		iv) Holdings of automatically discountable Storage Agency bill; working balances with the Treasury; and, until May 1969, Treasury bills redeemable on demand	12	–114	–11	—	53
		v) Liquid foreign exchange assets, freely repatriable and convertible into lire, given prevailing Bank of Italy directives[2]	159	–208	84	–117	25
III.	TOTAL USES OF MONETARY BASE (I + II)		1,241	1,245	2,155	3,312	23,258

1. Includes only those long-term bonds that, on specific occasions, were allowed to be substituted for cash and/or Treasury bills. Excludes long-term bonds allowed to be held as reserves against increases in time and savings deposits of commercial banks and against all deposits of savings banks (see Appendix A,I. for detailed explanation).
2. See Appendix A,II. for detailed explanation.

Source: Banca d'Italia, *Relazione Annuale* 1971, p. 213 (and similar tables in earlier reports).

(or aggregate changes in the forms in which it is held) has little causal significance for economic behaviour; in the very short run currency held by the non-bank public largely adjusts to current income, while bank reserves are linked to the future credit potential of the commercial banks. Any behavioural interpretation of the uses of monetary base therefore requires disaggregation of these heterogeneous components.

While the discussion in the preceding paragraph looks at the uses of the base, i.e. the forms in which it is held, it is also possible— and more relevant from a policy viewpoint— to analyse observed changes in the base by the factors which created them. Looked at from *the sources* side, changes in the base are created by imbalances in the net payments between, on the one hand, the Italian private sector and, on the other hand, the rest of the world and the government, corrected for various transactions by the monetary authorities. The sources of change in the monetary base have traditionally been disaggregated not only according to the three-fold institutional distinction between the possible counterparts to the private sector transactions, but also into those factors which are predominantly under the control of the monetary authorities and other ("autonomous" or "market") factors. It is, however, rather arbitrary where one draws the line between autonomous and policy-induced creation of monetary base. Even in the case of changes in borrowing at the Bank of Italy, which by definition is classified among the policy factors, the initiative may come from the private banks in the form of a repayment, because the demand for bank credit is slack. The total financing requirement of the Treasury is considered autonomous although it could typically not be allowed to be reflected fully in creation of base money— while the sale of bonds which contributes to meeting the requirement is considered to be entirely a policy factor. Because the distinction between autonomous and policy factors may convey somewhat inaccurate notions about the policy options available, the Bank of Italy has recently ceased to show it in the tables of the Annual Report.

The composition of the sources of monetary base creation into net payments from the rest of the world and the Treasury and Bank of Italy credit shows that total quarterly changes in the base have generally fluctuated much less than the individual sources (Chart 2). This tendency towards offset would be clearer in data relating to periods shorter than a quarter; it is an important function of a central bank in Italy as elsewhere to offset short-run and seasonal fluctuations in liquidity. Flexibility in short-run monetary management has been particularly important in Italy because of sharp seasonality and the unpredictability of the outturn of the public finances. Over quarters Bank of Italy credit has at times tended to mitigate some of the volatility of the impact from the foreign sector; the clearest example of this occurred during the 1962-64 turnaround in the balance of payments. In recent years, with the mounting budget deficits, the Treasury has become the most important source of base creation and some offset through a reduction in Bank of Italy credit appeared desirable. Such offsetting operations are, however, only part of the tasks of the monetary authorities; there have been marked shifts in the overall rate of monetary base creation which may be attributed to changes in the basic stance of policy. The causes of such changes and their timing are reviewed in Part III. Finally, it must be recalled that although the main interest in Italy focuses on the total creation of monetary base, there

28

is some reason to believe that the composition of the sources is of interest in itself, in that their further impact on domestic credit flows is not identical (see notably page 48).

The Italian authorities saw some advantages in formulating their policies with respect to the monetary base rather than the earlier used concept of excess reserves. Some of the evidence relevant to this point is reviewed in Part III. But it may already be noted here that the main advantage was that the link from the base to the monetary aggregates appeared to be more stable than that from the small and erratic excess reserves to these aggregates.[1] The 1965 changes in reserve requirements further blurred any causal interpretation of movements in excess reserves. An additional point in favour of the base was that it could be more closely controlled by the authorities than excess reserves which are also under the influence of the behaviour of the banks and the non-bank public.[2] But the practical difference of moving from one concept to the other must not be exaggerated since in the shorter run sharper changes in the base are bound to be strongly reflected in excess reserves. This fact as well as the gradual substitution of one concept for another appears to make it legitimate to describe policy for the whole of the period since the early 1960s in terms of developments in the monetary base.

The Italian monetary authorities do not formulate short-run operating targets for the monetary base. In contrast to the formulation in some other countries, notably the United States, of rather precise guidelines for what is thought to be desirable developments in short-term interest rates, bank reserves and monetary aggregates, the formulation of targets for monetary base creation in Italy refers to years rather than months or quarters. This lack of emphasis on the short run is seen to be justified by the rather long time lags with which changes in the base affect bank credit (pp. 45-46). Annual targets have been made in recent years; they have been published *inter alia* in the Bank of Italy Annual Reports since 1968. A preliminary formulation of a target for a calendar year is prepared at a meeting of the Interministerial Committee held during the preceding summer. The target is reformulated in the publication by the Ministry of the Budget shortly before the beginning of the year and once more in the Annual Report of the Bank of Italy which appears in May. Thus the annual targets— which at times involve looking up to 18 months ahead—

---

1. This argument was initially made by several academic economists in criticism of the prominent role of net free reserves in the formulation of monetary policy in the United States; see notably K. Brunner and A. Meltzer, "Some Further Investigations of Demand and Supply Functions for Money", *The Journal of Finance*, May 1964.

2. One further advantage of using the base rather than excess reserves, viz. that information about developments in the base is available without delay whereas movements in reserves become known only at monthly reporting dates, does not arise in the case of Italy. The definition of the base includes postal deposits and the — occasionally substantial— shifts between these and deposits with the commercial banks only become known with some time lag. Indeed, the substitutability of the two types of deposits would make it useful to regard postal deposits as part not of the base itself, but only of a broader monetary aggregate. The reason why this is not done is that postal deposits provide Treasury financing; if the public shifts out of them, financing requirements in other forms, notably Bank of Italy credit, increase. The inclusion of postal deposits therefore makes possible a more adequate analysis of the role of Treasury financing as a source of monetary base creation.

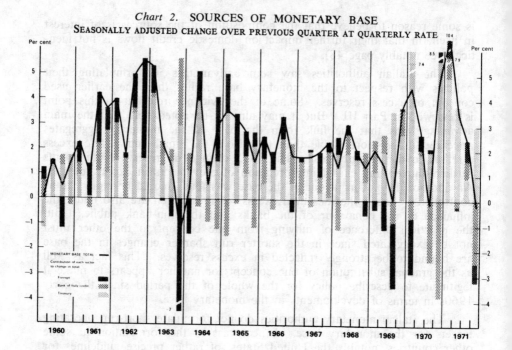

Chart 2. SOURCES OF MONETARY BASE
SEASONALLY ADJUSTED CHANGE OVER PREVIOUS QUARTER AT QUARTERLY RATE

are regularly revised; and between such revisions they serve as a rough framework for shorter-term decisions, notably relating to the financing of government deficits (page 22).

The procedure used in formulating annual targets may be summarized in the following way: on the basis of projections of (real and nominal) GNP— the responsibility for which lies with the semi-official Institute for Conjunctural Studies (ISCO) rather than with the Bank of Italy— and the investment component therein, the demand for credit in all forms, bank loans and securities, at existing levels of interest rates is estimated. If the level of GNP envisaged does not deviate from what is considered desirable, it is possible to calculate the amount of monetary base which has to be supplied to enable the banks to support the anticipated credit-deposit expansion, taking into account any drain into currency holdings by the public. The estimated demand for bonds by the banks and the non-banking public will then determine the volume of new security issues that can be authorised without changing the prevailing level of long-term interest rates. However, the projected developments for GNP may be unsatisfactory or they might fail to materialize, as has indeed been the case on several occasions in recent years, where the strength of demand has tended to be over-estimated. In such a situation the monetary authorities are faced with the problem of assessing how rapid a growth rate of the monetary base and/or what level of long-term interest rates will be required to stimulate initially financial, but ultimately real demand back to desired levels. The results of research done in the Bank of Italy and

30

Chart 3.   MONETARY BASE, DOMESTIC CREDIT AND MONEY SUPPLY (M₂)

SEASONALLY ADJUSTED 3-PERIOD MOVING AVERAGES;
CHANGE OVER PREVIOUS QUARTER AT ANNUAL RATE

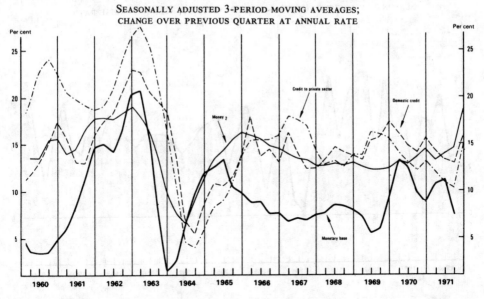

elsewhere show (see Part IV) that the empirical knowledge necessary for answering this type of question remains rudimentary.

While the monetary base has become the main target for the Italian monetary authorities, this should not be taken to imply that there was little concern about movements in market interest rates. In fact, long-term bond rates were remarkably stable until 1969, with the only sizeable change taking place in 1963-64. The period mid-1966 to mid-1969 was the extreme experience; during this three-year period long-term bond rates (on both government and corporate bonds) hardly varied. The Bank of Italy made known its intention to stabilize rates in the face of the rapidly rising supply of bonds arising out of the Treasury borrowing requirements (page 22). In retrospect, the period of pegging did not require large-scale open market operations and wider fluctuations in the creation of monetary base; indeed, the growth rate of the latter was smoother during 1966-69 than in the rest of the 1960s (see Charts 2 and 3)[1]. This is not as surprising as it may appear, because monetary policy in this period was not used for the purpose of "fine tuning" of an economy close to supply-demand balance. The period of pegging cannot be understood solely in the context of short-run demand management. By announcing their intention to keep bond rates stable the authorities increased the attractiveness of bonds relative to other financial assets. Thus it was designed to increase the scope for selling bonds to the private sector, a task in which it was successful.

1. At least one study suggests that the monetary projections of the Bank of Italy were facilitated by the introduction of pegging, see A. Fazio and P. Savona, "Pegging of Long-term Rate, Inflation and the Control of Credit Supply in an Open Economy", Draft for Second Konstanz Seminar on Monetary Theory and Policy, June 1971 (to be published).

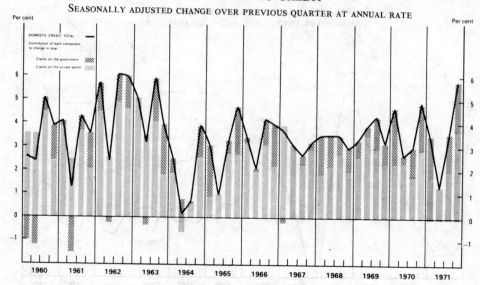

Chart 4. DOMESTIC CREDIT

SEASONALLY ADJUSTED CHANGE OVER PREVIOUS QUARTER AT ANNUAL RATE

Such structural considerations have played a role also in shaping the design of other modifications of policy instruments, e.g. in the easing of reserve requirements (see page 23). The period of pegging is only the clearest of several illustrations of the dual nature of Italian monetary policy during the period under study: a permanent concern to widen the flow of long-term finance through the bond market, but modified by the need to apply the monetary instruments vigorously in periods of inflation and/or balance of payments deficits.

In conclusion, the preference for formulating monetary policy for domestic stabilisation in terms of the monetary base has not been a rigid one. In fact, the authorities have adopted a pragmatic approach to the formulation of policy and paid due attention to the developments of market interest rates. This attitude seems to have reflected the fact that little detailed work has been possible on the relative importance of interest rates and monetary and credit aggregates in the determination of private expenditures. Flexibility in the policy formulation has been all the more relevant as it has not yet been made clear whether a quantity variable (i.e. monetary base) matters more than interest rates in the achievement of the external balance (the balance on non-monetary transactions and its financing), a policy objective of the Italian authorities as important as domestic economic stabilization. In this respect, it should also be noted that direct controls on the banks' foreign positions and on security issues on foreign capital markets have at time been used for the adjustment of the balance of payments.

III

THE USE OF MONETARY POLICY
AND ITS IMPACT ON FINANCIAL VARIABLES

The present part describes briefly the cyclical context in which monetary policy was used, identifies the main policy phases and assesses the
impact on financial variables, in so far as the latter is possible. The
dating of the policy phases will be based partly on observed developments
in the monetary base, but this in itself is not adequate, since two of the
phases are characterised more by changes in interest rates than by any
significant variations in the rate of growth of the base. The assessment
of the impact on financial variables will be based on the elaborate financial
sector model constructed in the Bank of Italy, supplemented by other
available evidence, mainly relating to international capital flows.

a) THE IDENTIFICATION OF POLICY PHASES AND THEIR BACKGROUND

For the purposes of the present study the period 1960-71 may be
sub-divided into seven policy phases. The first— beginning 1960 to end
1961— and the last— after the third quarter of 1970— will only be
reviewed in very broad terms. The late period is typically not yet included
in the financial and real impact relationships available and the early period
is relatively uneventful; it may be characterised by an accommodating
policy stance with accelerating growth rates for the monetary base to
prevent the liquidity position of the commercial banks from declining too
sharply in the face of a rapid rise in money incomes and credit demand.
This leaves five policy periods which in the briefest terms may be classified
as follows:

  i)   beginning 1962 to mid-1963: expansionary;
  ii) third quarter 1963 to first quarter 1964: disinflationary;
  iii) second quarter 1964 to mid-1966: reflationary;
  iv) mid-1966 to mid-1969: accommodating (with pegging);
  v)   mid-1969 to third-quarter 1970: moderately restrictive.

The developments in the sources and uses of the monetary base during
these five policy phases are shown in Tables 7 and 8; and the simulta-
neous trends in domestic credit and in money supply broadly defined (M_2)
are reported in Table 9. Visual impressions of these developments may
be obtained from Charts 3 and 4, while Chart 5 looks at the movements in
bank liquidity (excess reserves, borrowing at the Bank of Italy and the
difference between them, net free or net borrowed reserves) and Chart 6

TABLE 7. SOURCES OF B.

	1st January 1962 30th June 1963 (6 quarters)		1st July 1963 31st March 1964 (3 quarters)	
	A *Billion Lire*	B %	A *Billion Lire*	B %
1. Foreign sector	460	5.6	−1,253	−12.5
2. Treasury	713	8.6	760	7.8
3. Bank of Italy credit to:				
i) Banking system	281[2]	3.4	481	4.9
ii) Others[3]	−27	−0.4	51	0.4
4. Total	1,427	17.0	39	0.4

1. Columns A show average annual rates of change in billions of lire derived from stock figures seasonally adjusted by the Secretariat. Columns B show average annual rate of growth of total stock (line 4), and contribution of each component to this total; because the rates are compounded quarterly, there are small discrepancies between line 4 and the sum of the components.

2. Adjusted to include 200 billion lire of monetary base effectively created in January 1952 as a result of the reduction in required reserves from 25 per cent to 22½ per cent.

TABLE 8. USES OF B.

	1st January 1962 30th June 1963 (6 quarters)		1st July 1963 31st March 1964 (3 quarters)	
	A *Billion Lire*	B %	A *Billion Lire*	B %
1. Held by non-banks	785	9.5	503	4.8
2. Held by banks	642	7.8	−464	−4.4
i) Required reserves	430[2]	5.3	91	0.8
ii) Excess reserves	212	2.8	−555	−5.4
3. Total	1,427	17.0	39	0.4
4. *Memorandum item:*				
Effective marginal deposit multipliers[3]		5.25[4]		11.90

1. Columns A show average annual rates of change in billion lire derived from stock figures seasonally adjusted by the Secretariat. Columns B show average annual rate of growth of total stock (line 3), and contribution of each component to this total; because the rates are compounded quarterly, there ares mall discrepancies between line 3 and the sum of the components.

2. Adjusted to include 200 billion lire of monetary base effectively created in January 1962 as a result of the reduction in the required reserves from 25 per cent to 22½ per cent.

at interest rates. The dating of the policy periods is, however, mainly justified by the movements in the monetary base and by the announced actions of the authorities. A brief characterisation of the background to the policy phases and the actions taken must now be attempted as an introduction to a discussion of the effects of monetary policy. The main policy measures are listed in chronological order in Appendix B.

1st April 1964 30th June 1966 (9 quarters)		1st July 1966 30th June 1969 (12 quarters)		1st July 1969 30th September 1970 (5 quarters)	
A *llion Lire*	B %	A *Billion Lire*	B %	A *Billion Lire*	B %
558	5.3	61	0.4	−478	−3.0
813	7.4	628	4.6	2,312	14.2
−115	−1.2	399	3.0	−227	−1.5
−81	−0.8	2	—	−175	−1.1
1,175	10.8	1,090	7.8	1,432	8.7

3. Special credit institutions, and other Bank of Italy net claims on the non-bank, non-government sector. Derived residually.

Source: Bank of Italy.

SELECTED PERIODS[1]

1st April 1964 30th June 1966 (9 quarters)		1st July 1966 30th June 1969 (12 quarters)		1st July 1969 30th September 1970 (5 quarters)	
A *illion Lire*	B %	A *Billion Lire*	B %	A *Billion Lire*	B %
660	6.1	753	5.5	932	5.7
515	4.8	337	2.5	500	3.0
300	2.8	337	2.5	532	3.2
215	2.0	—	—	−32	−0.2
1,175	10.8	1,090	7.8	1,432	8.7
8.26		9.62		8.37	

3. Reciprocal of the ratio of the change in required reserves held in the form of monetary base during each time period to the change in total deposits during the corresponding period.
4. Adjusted for the effect referred to in footnote 2.

Source: Bank of Italy.

Expansionary phase. Beginning 1962 to mid-1963. This phase was preceded by three years of rapid economic expansion, a high degree of price stability and a surplus on current account; both wholesale and consumer prices did, however, begin to rise faster in the course of 1961 and continued accelerating for about two years. The labour market tightened as full employment was approached for the first time in the post-war

TABLE 9. DOMESTIC CRE

	1st January 1962 30th June 1963 (6 quarters)			1st July 1963 31st March 1964 (3 quarters)		
	A		B	A		B
	Billion Lire	%	%	Billion Lire	%	%
1. Total domestic credit[2]	2,844	20	20	3,052	18	18
of which:						
i) to the private sector	2,528	25	18	1,908	15	11
ii) to the government	316	8	2	1,144	28	7
2. Money supply (M_2)[3]	2,624	17	—	1,724	10	—

1. Columns A show average annual rates of change in billions of lire and in per cent derived from seasonally adjusted stock figures supplied by the IMF. Columns B show average annual rate of growth of total stock and contribution of each component to this total.

Chart 5. BANKS' LIQUID ASSETS AND CENTRAL BANK CREDIT TO BANKING SYSTEM

SEASONALLY ADJUSTED QUARTER-END DATA

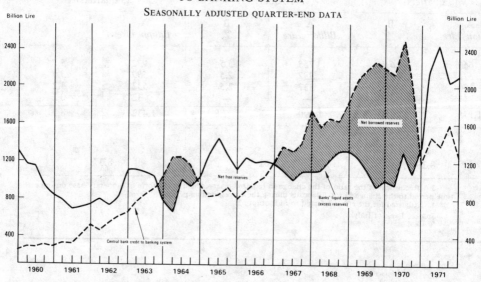

period and wage increases began putting pressure on enterprises' liquidity, already strained by heavy investment outlays. Fiscal policy was becoming gradually less contractionary. Throughout 1962 the current surplus was diminishing and the deterioration continued steadily after the surplus had disappeared around the end of the year. In the fall of 1962 and early

1st April 1964 30th June 1966 (9 quarters)			1st July 1966 30th June 1969 (12 quarters)			1st July 1969 30th September 1970 (5 quarters)		
A		B	A		B	A		B
illion Lire	%	%	*Billion Lire*	%	%	*Billion Lire*	%	%
,188	10	10	4,148	15	15	5,707	15	15
,504	10	7	3,228	15	12	3,770	13	10
684	13	3	920	12	3	1,937	20	5
,852	13	—	3,896	13	—	4,833	13	—

2. By banking system, including Bank of Italy, in the form of loans and securities.
3. Currency in circulation plus all demand and time deposits at banks.
Source: Bank of Italy.

1963 there was also some outflow of non-monetary capital, which appeared to be mainly due to special factors, notably a weakening of the confidence of Italian investors following the nationalisation of the electricity industry.

The stance of policy remained expansionary up to the third quarter of 1963. The Bank of Italy extended credit liberally to the commercial banks and reserve requirements were lowered at the beginning of 1962. Another important measure influencing the creation of monetary base was the abolition in November 1962 of the obligation on banks to maintain at least a net balanced position in foreign exchange vis-à-vis non-residents. With banks free to run an unlimited net debtor position, there was a massive inflow of banking funds which much more than offset the drain from the current account and non-monetary capital account. The foreign sector contributed along with the Treasury to the growth of the monetary base which was running at an annual rate of 17 per cent in the six quarters between the beginning of 1962 and the middle of 1963. This extremely rapid rate of base creation— unparallelled for any length of time during the period under study except for the 1970-71 recession— was seen at the time as a necessary risk. By thus leaving scope for the financing of the sharp increase in wages and other costs, the monetary authorities hoped to preserve high employment, thereby giving the newly formed coalition government (the first centre-left government) an opportunity to settle in. The deterioration of the balance of payments put an end to the expansionary policies before their potential effects could be assessed.[1]

---

1. The Bank of Italy has provided a detailed explanation of its policies i.e. in the 1962 *Annual Report;* see notably pp. 93-96 (english version). A criticism of the policies followed may be found in F. Modigliani and G. la Malfa, "Inflation, Balance of Payments Deficit and their Cure through Monetary Policy: the Italian Example", *Banca Nazionale del Lavoro Quarterly Review,* March 1967.

Disinflationary phase.   Third quarter 1963 to first quarter 1964.   The expansion of economic activity which had begun to lose momentum already in the first half of 1963— although this was not recognized at the time— slowed down markedly.   Investment in equipment appears to have reached its peak in the second quarter and the rate of increase in both wholesale and consumer prices tapered off from early 1963.   But the current account continued to deteriorate until near the end of the year and the outflow of non-monetary capital continued.   From sometime late in 1963, the current account began to recover sharply and by the first quarter of 1964 it was already nearly back in equilibrium.

Monetary policy was tightened sharply in September 1963 when a freezing of the net debtor position vis-à-vis non-residents was announced; earlier during the summer banks had been requested in less formal ways to stop increasing their foreign indebtedness.   The net foreign indebtedness ceiling was reduced at the beginning of 1964.   The monetary base remained very nearly constant during the three quarters as the large drain from the foreign sector was approximately offset by continuing substantial base creation via the Treasury accounts and a slightly faster growth rate in Bank of Italy credits to the commercial banks.   As currency holdings by the non-bank public continued to rise, monetary base available for the banks contracted sharply.   The restrictive management of the base was intended to be reinforced by the introduction in early 1964 of hire purchase regulations stipulating minimum down payments and maximum term on instalment purchases; but Parliament did not enact the necessary legislation until September 1964.

Reflationary phase.   Second quarter 1964 to mid-1966.   During the two years that followed, the current account improved continuously until mid-1965 and then stabilized at a high level of surplus of the order of 2-3 per cent of GNP.   The balance on non-monetary capital which was back in equilibrium in early 1964 worsened steadily over the two years, though still leaving a surplus on total non-monetary transactions towards the end of the phase.   Among the indicators of domestic demand, gross fixed investment continued to decline throughout 1964 and then stabilized at a level well below not only the 1963-average but also the 1962 level, until near the middle of 1966.   GNP, however, expanded steadily, pulled ahead by rapid growth of exports and some pick-up of consumption.   Fiscal policy which had been about neutral in 1964 became strongly expansionary in 1965, reaching in that year the maximum of its annual impact on GNP during the period under study (on the definition from the Hansen study of the fiscal impact) of more than 3 per cent of GNP.   The rate of increase of consumer prices slowed down steadily and was at the end of the period no faster than the 2-3 per cent per annum observed for wholesale prices.

With the indicators of demand pressure evidently weakening, a new policy phase was introduced during the second quarter of 1964.   The change of monetary policy was sharply reflected in the monetary base which increased at an accelerating rate from the end of the first quarter of 1964.   The additions to the base peaked in mid-1965 and from then the growth rate declined gradually; the average annual rate for the 9 quarters was close to 11 per cent.   With the foreign sector and the Treasury now both contributing to the creation of monetary base the Bank of Italy could, for the first time in the 1960s, reduce its volume of credit.   As

38

currency demand rose by only 6 per cent per annum— somewhat more slowly than nominal income which was rising at an annual rate of 8-9 per cent— the commercial banks swung into a positive net reserves position at the end of 1964 and remained positive until end-1966 despite some further tightening of the required net foreign position. Reserve requirements were eased in two stages (October 1964 and September 1965); particularly important was the easing of the requirements against commercial banks' time and savings deposits which could, from October 1965, be met by holding certain categories of long-term bonds instead of base money. The hire purchase restrictions which had been belatedly enacted in late 1964 were modified before the end of that year and suspended soon thereafter.

Accommodating phase (with pegging). Mid-1966 to mid-1969. It may be argued that the grounds for distinguishing between a reflationary phase up to mid-1966 and an accommodating one thereafter are tenuous. Indeed the thrust of policy was modified rather than changed; but the techniques used in monetary policy were partly new and appear to merit separate treatment. Real developments were also somewhat different, mainly in that gross fixed investment finally picked up from mid-1966 and continued a steady rise for nearly three years, though the 1963 investment peak was only surpassed in late 1967. Price increases were on the whole very moderate until early 1969 and the rate of growth of real output steady at about 6 per cent annually, or slightly faster than the growth of potential output. The current account surplus continued at a remarkably stable level while the deficit in the balance on non-monetary capital appeared to stabilise in 1966-67; but from early 1968 it began to increase at an accelerating pace. Fiscal policy had a strong restraining influence in 1967 and an almost equally large expansionary effect in 1968, both apparently larger than intended.

In terms of developments in the monetary base, the three-year period taken as a whole marked a slight deceleration to an annual growth rate of nearly 8 per cent. The expansionary impact from the foreign sector nearly vanished and that from the Treasury also weakened; the expansion of Bank of Italy credit therefore had to be resumed to assure an adequate growth rate for the case. But the reason for separate treatment of this three-year period is the introduction, in the course of the second quarter of 1966, of a policy of nearly completely stable bond rates. The stabilisation of the bond rate implied some modification in the formulation of policy (pp. 31-32); but this was also the period in which annual targets for monetary base creation found their way into the Bank of Italy's Annual Reports. The expectation was that the Bank of Italy might have to support the bond market extensively in the face of rapidly mounting public expenditures. This turned out to be unnecessary, partly because large shortfalls in public investment expenditures delayed public issues, partly because both commercial banks and the non-bank public showed a greater readiness than anticipated to absorb new issues. Towards the end of the accommodating phase monetary policy was gradually changing; to neutralize the effects on the base of the net outflow on non-monetary capital, banks were instructed to reduce their net asset position vis-à-vis non-residents, but since this and other measures only took effect from mid-1969 it seems justified to date the beginning of the next policy phase from that time.

Chart 6. INTEREST RATES
QUARTERLY AVERAGES

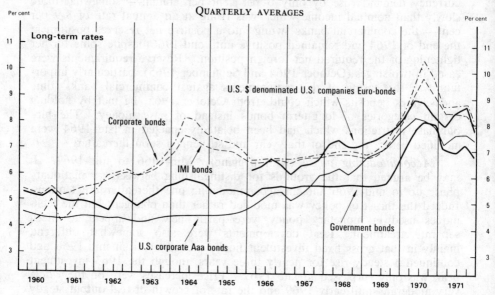

Per cent — Long-term rates

U.S. $ denominated U.S. companies Euro-bonds

Corporate bonds

IMI bonds

Government bonds

U.S. corporate Aaa bonds

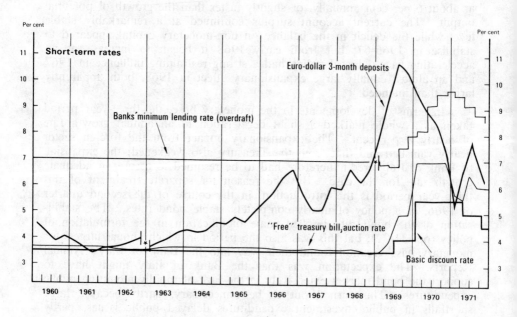

Per cent — Short-term rates

Euro-dollar 3-month deposits

Banks' minimum lending rate (overdraft)

"Free" treasury bill, auction rate

Basic discount rate

Moderately restrictive phase. Mid-1969 to the third quarter of 1970. As in 1963, the main element in the real background to the change in monetary policy was a sharp deterioration in the balance of payments. The current account surplus began to decline sharply from early in 1969 and although the worsening of the non-monetary capital account was brought to a stop around that time, the overall balance on non-monetary transactions was in substantial deficit throughout 1969. Prices had already begun to accelerate from late 1968; and, finally, widespread strikes led to a substantial loss of output in the third quarter— the "hot autumn"— of 1969. Although domestic demand appeared to recover quickly in the first few months thereafter, industrial production flattened out from the spring of 1970 while consumer prices continued to rise much faster than in earlier years.

Monetary policy was changed in the second quarter of 1969 at first, as before, by attempts to offset the outflow of non-monetary capital by instructing banks to reduce from the middle of the year their net foreign asset position. The auction rate for Treasury bills drifted up from April and shortly after the middle of the year the pegging of long-term government bond rates was abandoned and rates moved up over the following 12-month period by around two percentage points despite massive purchases by the Bank of Italy and tighter rationing of new issues. During the final stages of the period of pegging, Italian interest rates had fallen increasingly out of step with rates in other financial centres, notably in the Eurodollar market, and this upward pull, which was one major factor behind the outflow of funds, could no longer be disregarded. The discount rate was raised in August for the first time in the 1960s, and in March 1970, when there were signs of a strong pick-up in demand, by a further step of 1.5 percentage points. Bank excess reserves reached historically low levels in May, but picked up sharply from June. The uncertainties in the economy caused some wavering in policy, but the statements by the authorities as well as the sharp increase in interest rates and the slowing down of total credit flows— bond issues plus bank loans— makes it necessary to classify this policy phase as restrictive, though obviously less drastically so than 1963-64. The monetary base continued to expand at the same or even a slightly faster rate than in the period of pegging; this was due to the financing of the Treasury's massive borrowing requirements mainly by Bank of Italy purchases of government securities; the contributions from the foreign sector as well as from credits to the private banks were both negative.

After the third quarter of 1970. When it became abundantly clear that the economy was not on any firm upward trend, monetary policy gradually became more expansionary. The first steps towards lowering the cost of bank borrowing were taken by the Bank of Italy in January 1971 but the monetary base was expanding fast already from the last quarter of 1970; in the five quarters up to the end of 1971 it rose at an annual rate of close to 18 per cent, more than a doubling of the rate observed in the preceding, moderately restrictive, phase. The real economy remained very sluggish, total output at constant prices rising by only 1.5 per cent in 1971, while prices were increasing by 6-7 per cent; the current account surplus more than doubled, while the outflow of non-monetary capital remained heavy. Private gross fixed investment declined by 5 per cent and residential construction by no less than 12 per cent in 1971; it is obvious therefore that the substantial increase in credit flows was used by borrowers to build up liquid rather than real assets.

Of the five phases singled out above, two have been classified as period of monetary restraint. Measured by developments in the monetary base, the 1963-64 phase marked a sharper swing in policy than the later (moderately) restrictive period, but the increase in interest rates was more pronounced in the later period. The three other phases, despite the diffe-

41

rent labels that have been put on them, superficially have much in common, though the growth of the monetary base was twice as fast in the first phase as in the third and fourth phases. The difficulty in describing these phases is in giving an adequate account of the background developments in the real economy. The launching of both periods of restraint were motivated by a sharp deterioration of the current balance of payments supplemented by substantial capital outflows; but the acceleration of prices was apparently a contributing factor. It is more difficult to ascertain from published statements or from the statistical series available whether other domestic indicators of the supply-demand balance played any important role in determining changes in monetary policy.

Since much of the discussion about Italian economic policy has in recent years centered on the failure to eliminate slack in the use of resources, it may be relevant, as a supplement and summary to this review of identifiable phases of monetary policy, to confront the dating of the restrictive phases with an indicator developed in the OECD Secretariat to assess in a rough way the balance between supply and demand in the non-agricultural sector of the Italian economy. This indicator, the GDP gap, shown in Chart 7 has been designed to measure the difference between potential and actual output; it offers an estimate— with the benefit of hindsight— of the unused capacity in the Italian economy, given the capital stock actually in existence.[1] The calculations are preliminary and more refined measures are in the process of being developed, notably in the Bank of Italy. Nevertheless, the gap indicator seems to provide a background for assembling how the various policy phases fitted into the needs of short-run demand management.

The GDP gap series gives a somewhat different dating of periods of demand pressure than the impressions conveyed by straightforward observation of the growth rates for major components of demand. Thus the GDP gap widened in the course of 1963 when additions to the capital stock were being made at a rapid pace; but at this time the more readily observable indicators of demand pressure were still pointing towards increasing strain. The other main difference between the gap and alternative demand pressure indicators is the apparent marked reduction of the gap, over the 1965-69 period, which is not reflected in the price and balance of payments statistics until around the turn of the year 1968-69.

The present section has briefly surveyed when and how monetary policy was changed for purposes of demand management in Italy. Although no systematic discussion of how the monetary authorities have reacted to observed changes in policy objectives is possible on the basis of available

---

1. "Potential output" is here defined as a level of output sustainable in the medium run and associated with an "optimal" use of productive resources. The tentative figures shown in Chart 7 are obtained by applying the coefficients derived from a simple Cobb-Douglas production function estimated over the 1959-70 years to "full employment" values of capital and labour. The "potential" input of capital is measured as the stock in existence multiplied by 0.94 (a high but not maximum rate of utilisation observed in the period under study), while "potential" labour inputs are derived from an employment function containing output, lagged employment and the capital utilisation rate as explanatory variables. It should be noted that the concept of "potential" labour inputs used here does not correspond to the full utilisation of all Italian labour reserves (including disguised unemployment in agriculture and emigrant workers), but is defined in a more restrictive sense as the labour force which could be fully employed by a given (and insufficient) capital stock.

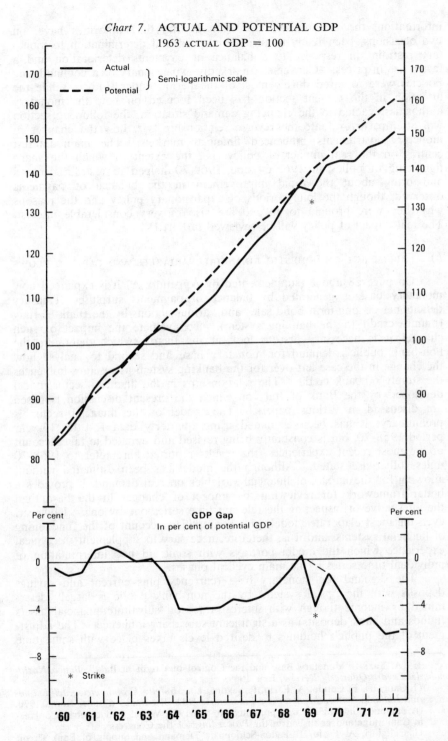

Chart 7. ACTUAL AND POTENTIAL GDP

1963 ACTUAL GDP = 100

Actual
Potential } Semi-logarithmic scale

GDP Gap
In per cent of potential GDP

Per cent

* Strike

'60 '61 '62 '63 '64 '65 '66 '67 '68 '69 '70 '71 '72

Source: Secretariat estimates; see footnote 1, page 42.

information, the preliminary impression is that the authorities have, on two occasions, been ready to turn with speed and determination to monetary restraint in response to a balance of payments deterioration and a faster rise in prices. Conversely, markedly expansionary or accommodating policies were followed during most of the period under study. While the attention in the present section has been focused on how the monetary authorities reacted to the changing demand situation, the following section will attempt to evaluate the reverse relationship, viz. how the changes in monetary instruments influenced financial markets. The main interest centres on the real impact of policy, i.e. the extent to which the sharp tightening of policy in 1963-64 and 1969-70 helped to restrain demand and bring about the rapid improvement in the balance of payments observed, though the long periods of expansionary policy and the reasons why they were brought to an end are also of very considerable interest. The real impact of policy will be reviewed in Part IV.

b) THE IMPACT ON DOMESTIC FINANCIAL VARIABLES AND CAPITAL FLOWS

On page 28 above (supplemented by Appendix A) it is explained how monetary base is generated by balance of payments surpluses, Treasury deficits net of long-term bond sales and various actions by the Bank of Italy (mainly credit to the banking system). To evaluate the impact of such changes it is necessary first to look at the factors which determine the non-bank public's demand for monetary base and second to analyse how the change in the case left over for the banking system as reserves influences the supply of bank credit. The relationships in the financial sector model developed by the Bank of Italy on which the present discussion is based are discussed in various papers.[1] The model of the financial sector is preliminary: it has been estimated using quarterly data for the 13-year period 1958-70, but is constantly being revised and updated to take account of the most recent experiences; the results reported here refer to 1958-70 unless otherwise stated. Although the model has been estimated without allowing for the impact of financial variables on real demand, it provides a better framework for reviewing the impact of changes in the base than the alternative of inspecting the relevant time series one by one. However, even the most elaborate models give a simplified account of the functioning of financial systems, and it is, therefore, necessary to supplement the typical experience which the model portrays with some ad hoc interpretation of individual time series in the main cyclical phases.

The demand for monetary base (currency plus current and savings deposits with the postal system) by the non-bank public is largely determined by income though with interest rates on substitute financial assets (bonds and bank deposits) as a significant subsidiary influence. The adjustment of the public's holdings to desired levels takes place with some time

---

1. A. Fazio: "Monetary Base and the Control of Credit in Italy", *Banca Nazionale del Lavoro Quarterly Review,* June 1969.

G. Caligiuri, F. Cotula, A. Fazio, P. Savona: *Un Modello Econometrico dell'Economia Italiana, Settore Monetario e Finanziario* (M1 BI), Banca d'Italia, Roma 1970. (A summary in English was presented at the 1970 World Econometric Congress in Cambridge and published in the *Proceedings* of the Congress).

G. Caligiuri, A. Fazio, T. Padoa-Schioppa: "Demand and Supply of Bank Credit in Italy", *Journal of Money, Credit and Banking* (forthcoming).

lag.   The implication of the findings is that in Italy, as in most other countries, bank reserves initially bear nearly the full brunt of changes in the monetary base.   As a first approximation income may be regarded as unrelated to current and immediate past changes in the base, and even when this is not the case, because some of the changes in the base are directly elements of income generation, the absorption of base outside the system will only be a small fraction of income especially in the first one or two quarters.   This simple picture is slightly modified if large interest rate changes occur, but in the following discussion this complication is ignored.

The interest therefore centres on the response of the banks to changes in their reserve position, i.e. the rate at which they acquire bonds and lend.   A research paper by F. Caligiuri and T. Padoa-Schioppa of the Bank of Italy is based on the useful simplification of lumping together bond holdings and direct lending in a supply function for bank credit.   This is a remarkable assumption in view of the different characteristics of the two assets with respect to both risk and return characteristics.   Changes in total bank earning assets[1] are explained primarily by current and past values of non-borrowed reserves and by interests rates, the latter being represented alternatively by long-term bond rates and by weighted averages of bond and loan rates.[2]

The main finding is that the direct effect of an increase in non-borrowed reserves viewed in isolation is to increase the supply of bank credit in the sense defined above by approximately seven times the change in reserves.   The process takes 5 to 6 quarters at a steady pace.   The credit multiplier has shifted upwards after the lowering of effective reserve requirements in 1965; before that it was around four.   The long period of adjustment of bank earning assets explains why the ratio of changes in bank earning assets to current or immediately preceding changes in the monetary base (or bank reserves) is highly unstable.   Changes in bank credit in any particular quarter must be seen as the result of an adjustment to the changes in the base in the five or six preceding quarters.   This view supplies the rationale for both the adherence of the Bank of Italy to the monetary base approach as a framework for policy decisions over a medium-term horizon such as a year and the reluctance to formulate precise shorter-run targets for the base (see page 29).[3]

The credit multiplier reviewed above is only a theoretical one as it is valid only when interest rates remain constant.   In fact, they will fall as the creation of monetary base accelerates and rise as it decelerates.   The Bank of Italy may directly lower rates to the extent that it injects monetary base through open market purchases; and in any case the acquisition of earning assets by the banks will tend to lower rates.   Since the willingness

---

1.   Since bank reserves are typically also interest-bearing, this terminology may be slightly inappropriate.

2.   In recent versions of the credit supply function, borrowed reserves (from the Bank of Italy or abroad) are also included as an explanatory variable.   Since bank borrowing largely takes the form of rediscounting, at the discretion of the Bank of Italy, of credit which might not have been extended in the absence on rediscounting facilities, changes in borrowing are regarded by the authors of the model as exogenous and as having a multiplier of one.   This assumption seems to require further discussion; it is probable that it imparts an upward bias in the estimate of the multiplier.

3.   This point is made strongly by Caligiuri, Fazio and Padoa-Schioppa, *op. cit.*

of banks to hold reserves is very significantly influenced by the level of interest rates— a one percentage point decrease in interest rates tends to lower the supply of bank credit by 2,000 billion lire— this response of interest rates acts as an important damper on credit expansion.

A complete picture of what happens in the market for credit in response to the manipulation of monetary base by the authorities thus requires some analysis of the demand for credit, here measured as the sum of bank loans and net increase in bonded indebtedness of the private non-bank sector. In making this analysis the financial sector model assumes interest rates to move in such a way as to clear the market for credit, so that actually observed combinations of credit flows and interest rates quarter by quarter are in equilibrium. This is a rather extreme assumption, though the evidence for rationing is not strong, except possibly in 1970. The analysis is also a simplification in the sense that it leaves out any possible impact from credit flows and interest rates on private expenditures and the repercussions of such an impact on financial variables, but since the response of the real sector to monetary changes is likely to occur only with some time lag, the bias resulting from this omission should not be large. The most important properties of the demand for credit function from the present point of view, then, is its sensitivity to interest rates; calculations suggest that a one percentage point decrease in interest rates typically increased the private sector demand for credit by close to 500 billion lire. The lower interest sensitivity in demand than in supply means that changes in the base will result in much smaller changes in the observed volume of credit than suggested by the credit multiplier calculation, and in substantial changes in interest rates. This conclusion which is of considerable relevance for the evaluation of a policy conducted primarily by manipulating the monetary base is demonstrated with more precision in the technical note at the end of the present Part.

It is possible to relate in a rough way this schematic view of the operation of the credit market to the order of magnitude of the changes in policy in the two phases of monetary restraint. In the 1963-64 phase, the growth of the monetary base was reduced to zero while open market operations remained negligible. Had the base been allowed to continue to expand at around 15 per cent, i.e. close to the very high rate observed during the previous expansionary phase, it would have been around 700 billion lire higher at the end of the restrictive phase than it actually was, implying, with the then prevailing multiplier of about four, an inward shift in the supply of credit of the order of 3,000 billion lire. Assuming the private non-bank sector's credit demand curve initially unchanged, the short-fall in the observed volume of credit was much smaller, possibly somewhat less than 1,000 billion lire. This is approximately consistent with the observed increase in long-term bond rates of one-and-a-half percentage point during this policy phase and the estimated interest sensitivity of credit demand and supply.

In the second restrictive phase it can hardly be claimed that the growth of monetary base was restricted severely; thus the supply function did not shift markedly. But long-term interest rates rose by about three percentage points in 1969-70, which in itself would tend to open up very considerable excess supply of credit; this effect was further reinforced by a small decline in the volume of government bonds supplied to the market. There is, however, no evidence of any excess supply arising,

46

because the demand curve for credit as measured here shifted strongly outwards at the same time; the excess demand for bonds by the non-banking public diminished sharply, and the demand for bank credit rose. The tighter regulation of new bond issues shifted some of the demand for credit towards the banks and some signs of rationing emerged in the summer of 1970 (see below).

In summary, the financial sector model is of help in interpreting more systematically events in financial markets during the two periods of active use of monetary policy. The most notable conclusion arising out of the rough illustrative description is the view of the transmission mechanism it implies rather than any numerical results. It is significant that the financial sector model views the scope for substitution in Italian financial markets as sufficiently close on both the assets and liabilities side to warrant aggregation of credit flows through the banks and the bond market. Interest rates also play a significant role in allocating financial saving between the main categories of assets: bonds, bank deposits and monetary base. That such a view is possible suggests a higher degree of perfection in the financial system than the apparent rigidity of bank lending and deposit rates and of the institutional structure in general would have led one to assume. It further implies that interest rate changes are an important element in the transmission mechanism from monetary policy instruments to the ultimate domestic targets, possibly more important than the availability effects often underlined in official statements in Italy.

There are some further elements from the model relating to supply of bank credit and to the external role of interest rates which need to be considered. The first point relates to the interpretation of the limited evidence available on the presence of rationing elements in the supply of bank loans. In research done at the Bank of Italy on the market for bank loans some attention has been devoted to developing tests for possible changes in the degree of credit rationing in 1963-64 ·and 1969-70.[1] The results which rely on a study of imperfections in interest rate adjustment during the two restrictive phases are not very significant; no evidence of rationing is found for the early restrictive phase but there are indications of an increasing degree of rationing early in 1970. This impression is confirmed by looking at data on the distribution of loans by size which is thought to be a useful indicator of changes in rationing, as the share of small size loans is likely to fall in periods of monetary restraint. The data have been collected in recent years by the Central Risks Office and commented upon in the two latest Annual Reports of the Bank.[2] In the first three quarters of 1970 there is a clear slowdown in the growth of total loans combined with an increase in the share of the largest loans which by the third quarter accounted for very nearly all of the new loans granted. In the fourth quarter of 1970 both tendencies were sharply reversed when the restrictive policies were brought to an end.

It must be pointed out that this indirect evidence on changes in credit availability at best gives as impression of the rationing of bank loans. Whether this type of rationing has effects on real demand depends on the scope the borrowers have for financing their activity by running down their financial assets and on the possibilities of substitution for the

---

1. See Caligiuri, Fazio and Padoa-Schioppa, *op. cit.*
2. See *Annual Reports* (english edition) of 1970, pp. 118-19, and 1971, p. 110.

47

unsatisfied borrowers through specialised credit institutions— the bond market is hardly a direct alternative. But since both the lending of the specialized institutions and their access to the bond market are under the control of the Bank of Italy, the extent to which these substitution possibilities materialize is in principle dependent on policy attitudes. It is likely that the rationing of bank credit and, probably more important, tighter regulation of new issues, reinforced the degree of restraint expressed in the rising interest rates during the two restrictive phases and particularly in 1970.

A second refinement of the financial sector model relates to the demand for credit by the non-bank private sector; it suggests a high degree of substitutability of foreign for domestic credit. There is evidence that changes in the monetary base arising from net payments from the rest of the world shift the demand function around; the calculations suggest that such flows shift the equilibrium position in the Italian credit market to nearly the full extent of the flow, but there are reasons to believe that this may overstate the case. These results can be supplemented by evidence in the demand functions for various categories of financial assets that disaggregation by source of changes in the monetary base may be fruitful; net payments from the rest of the world or the Treasury increase in the short-run the readiness of the Italian non-bank sector to hold various categories of financial assets— postal deposits and bank demand deposits— beyond the levels that other determinants, i.e. income and interest rates, would indicate. To the extent that such differential effects are important they make short-run monetary management, solely in terms of aggregate changes in the base an over-simplification. Thus, in relations other than the credit supply function, the total change in the base— or rather in that part of it which accrues to the banks as reserves— has been found to be in need of disaggregation to serve as an explanatory variable. This underlines that from an operational point of view it is useful for the monetary authorities to have reliable information on present and future trends in those sources of base change not directly under control; otherwise it is not possible to offset or reinforce the impact from these sources in such a way as to keep total bank credit or other monetary aggregates close to a desired course.

On the whole, the financial sector model does not take systematically into account the interrelationships between Italian and foreign interest rates, while introducing the main items in the capital account of the balance of payments directly as exogenous variables. Although it can be shown that the Italian authorities have systematically offset a considerable part of the monetary base impact of the balance of payments (see page 50) a full understanding of the financial mechanism cannot be obtained by a model which is basically applicable to a closed economy.[1] Data deficiencies have precluded the estimation of a well-specified model of the Italian capital account on a quarterly basis.[2] Accordingly the quantitative evidence has

---

1. Even if the offset to the external impact on the monetary base were complete, the implication of the arguments above is that the external links cannot be disregarded.

2. A model has been formulated in some detail; see *Un Modello Econometrico dell'Economia Italiana (M1 BI) - Settore Rapporti Finanziari con l'Estero*, Banca d'Italia 1970. Here interest rates are tentatively assumed to influence direct foreign investment, portfolio investment and trade credits. The set of relationships for the external financial sector also includes equations determining the spot and forward exchange rates.

to be confined to either the total capital account or one major component thereof which is identifiable, viz. the export of lira bank notes, mainly to Switzerland. A detailed study of the regularities in the remittance of bank notes up to the end of 1969 has been published by Vicarelli,[1] who finds the growing volume of such flows to have been sensitive to variations in the differential between Italian long-term bond rates and the uncovered three-month Eurodollar rate. The sensitivity has been increasing strongly in the course of 1960s; the interest rate factor becomes rather dominant after 1966, although there is evidence that fiscal incentives and seasonal factors have also contributed.

A recent study by Branson and Hill has adopted a more aggregative approach to the explanation of Italian capital flows to circumvent the problem of data inadequacies.[2] Unfortunately this study of quarterly net capital flows in the 1960-69 period lumps together movements in banking and non-banking funds; but as no systematic account is taken of the shifting regulations pertaining to the net foreign position of the commercial banks, the estimates of interest sensitivity may be biased. The study suggests a considerable sensitivity to changes in the three-month Eurodollar deposit rate; a one percentage point increase in the latter rate, with Italian rates constant, could give rise to an outflow of nearly 250 billion lire in the course of six months. As the differential between the Eurodollar rate and the prime lending rate of Italian commercial banks widened by 3-4 per cent in the course of 1969, Branson and Hill's calculations suggest that this sharp shift in relative interest rates induced an outflow almost of the size of the normal annual additions to the monetary base. The effects of the increase in Italian rates and the decline in Eurodollar rates which followed also appear to have been sizeable; in the course of 1970 the capital account shifted from a deficit of 400 billion lire in the first quarter to a surplus of 270 billion lire in the fourth quarter of the year.

Apart from changes in interest rate differentials, the Branson and Hill study finds a systematic influence on net capital flows from excess saving in the Italian economy. When *ex ante* savings exceed investments, funds have tended to flow abroad; the net outflow has been significantly related to current and lagged value of the gap between potential and actual GNP. An excess supply of credit may not have been fully reflected in interest rates or in other financial indicators; this is a possible explanation of why the gap variable contributes to the explanation of capital flows (see also the results discussed on page 47). The findings of Branson and Hill suggest, in other words, that the substantial outflow of funds experienced in Italy, notably towards the end of the 1960s, had a macro-economic rationale in addition to the role of a widening interest rate differential in Italy's disfavour.

A recent paper by Kouri and Porter[3] adopts a somewhat different view of the mechanism generating capital flows than the portfolio balance

1. F. Vicarelli, "L'Esportazione di Bancnote nell'Esperienza Italiana dell'Ultimo Decennio", *Studi Economici* 1970.

2. W. Branson and R.D. Hill, Jr., "Capital Movements in the OECD Area: An Econometric Analysis", *OECD Economic Outlook, Occasional Studies,* December 1971.

3. P. Kouri and M. Porter, "International Capital Flows and Portfolio Equilibrium", paper presented to the annual meeting of Project Link, Vienna, September 1972. Permission to refer to this paper is gratefully acknowledged.

approach of Branson and Hill. The basic idea is that capital flows are generated primarily by an imbalance between the demand and supply of domestic money; if an excess demand for money is brought about by a tightening of monetary policy, part of the effects is offset by a net private capital inflow. The implication of this view is that net capital flows may be explained largely by changes in income and changes in the monetary base from sources other than capital flows; changes in the discount rate and in a representative foreign rate also play a part to the extent that they influence the composition of the equilibrium stock of financial assets between money, domestic bonds and foreign bonds. The empirical results of applying the Kouri-Porter model reinforce the impression from the Bank of Italy financial sector model referred to on page 48 that such close substitutability between Italian and foreign financial markets is a relevant view of the capital flow mechanism. Their calculations explain 75 per cent of the fluctuations in the net flow of private, non-monetary capital by quarters in the 7-year period 1964-70. A notable difference vis-à-vis the Branson and Hill study is the less significant role of changes in the Euro-dollar rate and the important role of changes in the level of Italian money income; in the absence of good quarterly income data, retail sales have been used as the main indicator of domestic transactions demand for money. Another interesting aspect of these results is the role of capital flows as an offset to other sources of base change; the offset to imbalances in the current account plus official capital flows is nearly complete (cf. the results of the credit demand relation reported on page 47) while a little more than half of the change in the Bank of Italy's net domestic assets (i.e. claims on the Treasury and the private sector) has typically been offset through the capital account. Thus, if the Bank of Italy were to decide to step up the increase in the monetary base by a given amount, the results suggest that it would have, in the short-run, to increase its domestic assets by a considerable greater amount thereby making room for an increased outflow of the same magnitude as the intended increase in the base.

It must be recalled that the Italian monetary authorities have devoted considerable attention to the latter problem of offsetting capital flows. They have done so primarily by changing the regulations pertaining to the net position of the banks vis-à-vis non-residents, a method which, as explained on page 24 and Appendix A, neutralises the impact of capital flows on both the monetary base and official international reserves. But in addition to this there are also indications that open market operations and lending by the Bank of Italy have tended to offset the impact on the base of movements of private non-banking funds.[1] This is not surprising in view of the typical characteristics of monetary base creation in Italy in recent years with persistent tendencies to large central government financial deficits and capital outflows. The use of the monetary base as the main operating target is also a factor which helps to explain why one should expect to find a rather clear tendency for domestic sources in the base to offset the fluctuations from capital flows.

---

1. See V. Argy and P. Kouri, "Sterlization Policies and the Volatility in International Reserves", International Monetary Fund (1972), forthcoming in R. Aliber (ed.) *National Monetary Policies and the International Monetary System*. This paper suggests that as much as 75 per cent of such movements tended to be offset by monetary policy in the 1963-70 period. Permission to refer to this paper is gratefully acknowledged.

The present survey of some important aspects of the way in which monetary base changes are transmitted to markets for bank loans and other forms of credit and how they interact with the capital account of the balance of payments tends to underline the mobility of funds both domestically and internationally. Although the Italian authorities have been well equipped to deal with the problem of offsetting capital flows, the strength of the links to other financial centres which emerges from the empirical studies, whether mainly relying on interest rates or not, has become such as to force an increasingly external orientation on short-run monetary policy. To what extent this creates a genuine dilemma situation for the Italian authorities depends on the role monetary policy can be expected to play in the attainment of domestic policy aims.

TECHNICAL NOTE TO PART III

The analysis of price formation in the credit market and the impact on the equilibrium position of a change in the monetary base may be given more precision with the help of Chart 8. The initial equilibrium position with a credit flow CR_0 and an interest rate i_0 refers to a period, say one year, sufficiently long to allow lagged adjustment effects to have settled on both sides of the market; and the same is the case for the new equilibrium. While the supply of credit comes from the banks, the demand for credit confronting it comes from the private non-bank sector, including

Chart 8. AN EQUILIBRIUM MODEL FOR THE CREDIT MARKET

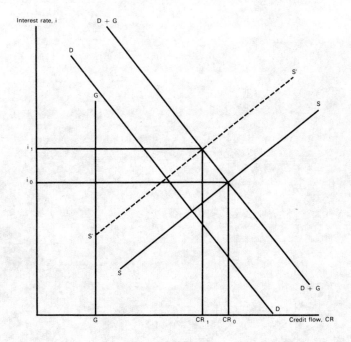

the specialised credit institutions, and from the Government. The private non-bank sector demands bank credit and is both a supplier and a demander of bonds; the curve DD refers to the sum of the demand for banks loans and the excess demand (typically negative) for bonds. The supply of government bonds is regarded as fixed and the initial equilibrium is under these assumptions indicated by the intersection of the aggregated credit demand curve $D+G$ and the bank supply function for credit SS, i.e. by a flow of credit CR_o at an interest rate i_o. There is now a reduction in the supply of monetary base— not linked to open market operations or debt management, since the supply of government bonds is assumed to be given— causing the supply of bank credit to shift inwards to S'S' by some multiple of the change in bank reserves, i.e. about seven times in the most recent period. If, among the determinants of the demand for bank credit, only interest rates change, the new equilibrium position is at the intersection of the stable demand curve and the new supply curve, i.e. at a credit flow of CR_1 and an interest rate i_1. As the results of the financial sector model suggest that the sensitivity of credit supply to interest rates is nearly four times as large as that of credit demand— a one percentage point increase in interest rates having typically been associated with a 500 billion lire decline in credit demand and a 2,000 billon lire increase in supply— the actual change in the volume of credit is much smaller than the shift in the supply curve, in the order of one fourth, and accompanied by a substantial change in interest rates.

IV

THE IMPACT OF MONETARY POLICY ON PRIVATE EXPENDITURES

The present part relates to the impact of monetary policy on the major components of domestic expenditures in Italy and on the ultimate objectives of policy: growth of real demand and employment as close as possible to the supply potential, price stability and balance of payments equilibrium. This is a difficult and controversial task in any economy, but even more so in the case of Italy for two main reasons:

i) The cyclical instability of the Italian economy has not been as pronounced as that observable in many other industrialised countries; the deceleration and irregularity of economic growth in recent years has mainly been due to persistent social tensions and political uncertainty, i.e. to factors other than those which are amenable to short-run demand management, including monetary policy. Thus, even if one had all imaginable information about short-term changes in the economy, it would be highly intricate to demonstrate how monetary policy has affected the course of output, employment and prices.

ii) The data for such a demonstration are in any case only partially available; while statistics relating to the financial sector are generally adequate, the use of data relating to the real economy requires serious qualifications. Many data are only available on an annual basis; changes in inventories, which in many economies, e.g. Japan, have been found to respond to monetary action, are not available at all.

For these reasons it is only possible to give preliminary impressions about how monetary policy has affected domestic demand. It is necessary to rely more on a basically subjective review of the time series for the main economic variables than was required in the evaluation of financial market effects where the empirical research makes quantitative illustrations possible. But the qualitative review will be supplemented by some references to the work on the real aspects of the Italian economy carried out in the Bank of Italy and at the University of Bologna. As in Part III, the main emphasis will be on the use of monetary policy in the two phases of restraint.

It must be recalled that the first of these two phases, mid-1963 to first quarter 1964, was shorter and possibly sharper than the mid-1969 to end-1970 period. In the early phase the creation of monetary base was brought to a near-complete halt; the deceleration of domestic credit and

53

of the money supply was sudden and initially to a large extent synchronous with that of the base, while long-term interest rates rose by about 1.5 percentage points. In the later phase of restraint there was little change in the growth of the monetary base— indeed, after a brief deceleration, it picked up again and averaged higher than for the previous, supposedly expansionary, phase— or in the trends for domestic credit and money supply; but there was a much sharper increase, approximately 3 percentage points, in long-term (and short-term) interest rates.

a) SOME EVIDENCE FROM PARTICULAR POLICY PHASES

The impact in the early phase of monetary restraint on credit flows, investment and the balance of payments was apparently rapid and has been generally viewed as a success for monetary policy. But it may well be asked whether the impact did not show up so quickly and strongly in the flow of credit (Table A4) that one would have to look also, or even primarily, to other determinants of investment and credit flows for an explanation of the sharp 1963-64 downturn. Investment in machinery and equipement (Chart 9 and Table A6) peaked in the second quarter of 1963, and stayed very close to the peak level until late that year; it then declined markedly in each of the following 5 quarters. Investment in the construction sector kept on rising moderately until the first quarter of 1964 and then declined moderately for 4 quarters. While these time patterns are generally consistent with the response of investment found in the econometric studies referred to below, the strength of the decline in machinery and equipment investment goes well beyond what could be expected from monetary factors. Other determinants of investment— value added and the share of profits therein— were also moving in this period in such a way as to bring about a fall in investment. The causal role of monetary restraint does not appear to have been dominant.

In the 1969-70 restrictive phase the tightening of policy took mainly the form of sharp rises in interest rates and some rationing, particularly in the bond market. The real impact of policy was apparently once more very sharp in both main categories of investment. Construction even declined erratically from the second quarter of 1969, just around the time when policy was tightened; a more substantial decline set in from the second quarter of 1970. But presumably these developments were influenced more by changes in legislation pertaining to urban developments than to the tightening of monetary policy. Investment in machinery and equipment fell rather sharply in the second half of 1969, but the main reason here was the unrest in labour markets culminating in widespread strikes late in the year. It was only from the end of 1970 that this category of investment showed a clear downward movement, but again rather stronger than can be justified as a delayed response to the tighter monetary policy in 1969-70.

It is generally believed that monetary policy works asymmetrically in the sense that it is more effective in restraining than in stimulating demand. Of the three expansionary phases of policy identified, two— before mid-1963 and mid-1966 to mid-1969— were characterised by generally smooth growth in the demand components susceptible to monetary influences; the 1967-68 moderate slowdown in investment seems primarily

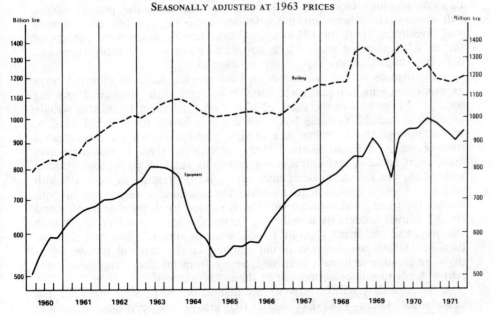

Chart 9. GROSS FIXED INVESTMENT
SEASONALLY ADJUSTED AT 1963 PRICES

to have been due to a deceleration of exports explained by recession in Germany. The phase, when there is a clear divergence between an expansionary monetary policy and its apparent effects, is in the period between the second quarter of 1964 and the introduction of the pegging regime in mid-1966. During this phase monetary policy was easy by any standard; but while the monetary aggregates picked up well from mid-1964, both main categories of investment fell until late 1964 and remained nearly flat for a year and a half thereafter. This sluggish response to a monetary stimulus was repeated even more clearly in the phase since the end of 1970 when both categories of investment have been declining in the face of a rapidly growing monetary base and receding bond rates.

b) SOME EVIDENCE FROM ECONOMETRIC MODELS

Unfortunately, the econometric results available are no more conclusive than the above summary review of the main components of private expenditure. At best, models can suggest some "typical" responses of real demand to variations in financial conditions. Asymmetries in responses to expansionary and restrictive policies may blur the meaning of what is "typical". Nevertheless, it may be useful to review the main empirical findings presently available. They include primarily the work in the Bank of Italy on a model with annual relationships for the period 1951-68, recently updated to include 1969-70, and a quarterly econometric model recently developed by a group of economists at the University of Bologna

55

and estimated on data for 1957-70 (56 quarters),[1] using the quarterly national accounts estimates by ISCO. In both cases the present review will concentrate strictly on the relations explaining private consumption and investment (both in 1963 prices), thus leaving aside most aspects of the models, including some which appear to be in a more satisfactory and definitive shape than the expenditure relationships.

As regards *private consumption* both models have in different ways experimented with a liquid asset variable to capture the impact of growing wealth. In the case of the Bank of Italy model the effect found was weakly established and the variable has been dropped in the most recent version. In the Bologna model there is a modest positive impact on consumption from increases in liquid assets. More surprisingly, there is also a positive association between consumption (or rather its ratio to disposable income) and the current long-term bond rate, although the presence of both a wealth and a cost effect should tend to make the association negative. In both models the main burden of explanation is carried by disposable income and (in the annual model) its distribution between wage and salary income on the one hand and other ("profit") income on the other. The fact that the data on private consumption is the residual in the national income identity— in the quarterly data even inseparable from inventory changes (Table A6)— tends to reduce confidence in the results derived.

As regards *fixed investment* no distinction is possible between the nationalised sector— ENEL, ENI, IRI etc.— and private enterprises; excluded from the measure used is only public works financed directly by government agencies. The annual data permit a breakdown between investment in industry, tertiary sectors and in housing. There is some evidence of a modest cost of capital effect on industrial investment besides the influence of capacity utilisation and value added. Very roughly, the relation suggests that an increase in the long-term bond rate of 1 percentage point tended towards the end of the 1960s to reduce fixed industrial investment by 60-70 billion lire in the course of a year— a modest effect since annual expenditures of this kind approached 4,000 billion lire (1963 prices) towards the end of the period.[2]

In explaining annual investment in housing, several experiments were made to allow for the influence of financial variables. The only variable which has a significant, though not strong, influence in the expected direction is the flow of loans from specialised credit institutions. But it may be recalled that these institutions supply only about half of the external

---

1. The main references are *Un Modello Econometrico dell'Economia Italiana (M1 BI), Settore Reale e Fiscale,* Bank of Italy, January 1970, and "Project Link, a Quarterly Econometric Model of the Italian Economy", Discussion Paper No. 7203, April 1972, Istituto di Scienze Economiche, University of Bologna, and mimeographed notes on the real model (M1, BI, RF4) from the Bank of Italy (1972). Permission from the authors of the two last unpublished papers to refer to their results is gratefully acknowledged.

2. This result is obtained by multiplying the estimated coefficient of .064 by the typical value added in industry, which approached 1,000 billion lire towards 1970. Since the weight of external finance was about half, this calculation assumes that the cost of internal funds rose in step with the bond rate; the illustrative result may therefore overstate the effect. No regard is paid to the role of tax factors in determining the cost per capita, but refinements in this area are underway, see i.a. Paola Savona, "Nota su una Stima del Costo del Capitale in Italia", Bank of Italy, February 1970.

finance for housing— or about 20 per cent of total finance— (page 15) and that these shares have been rather stable throughout the 1960s. Two other financial variables were tried, mortgage rates and changes in the public's holdings of bonds. The mortgage rate appears with a positive sign, which is contrary to what one would expect in an equilibrium model, but the finding might be justified as an indicator of rationing and delayed adjustment of mortgage rates. The influence of increases in the public's bond holding is negative i.e. also in the opposite direction of what one would expect. On the basis of these results it is not surprising that the easy monetary policy pursued since 1970 has been incapable of pulling residential construction out of its prolonged slump.

The quarterly investment relationships estimated in the Bologna model broadly confirm the conclusions of the annual model. A straight-forward comparison is not possible because a different breakdown of investment— into machinery and transportation equipment on the one hand and residential and industrial construction on the other— is imposed by the availability of quarterly statistics. No financial effects have been traced in the former of the two series, but there is a modest effect on total construction of changes in long-term interest rates lagged between one and eight quarters. According to this relationship, a 1 percentage point increase in the long-term bond rate would entail a reduction of investment in fixed and industrial construction of nearly 140 billion lire over a two-year period. About 8 per cent of this total effect would come in the quarter following that with the change in interest rates; 15-20 per cent of the total effect would come in each of the next four quarters, after which the effects gradually taper off. This category of investment was running at a rate of about 5,000 billion lire annually, so that the first-year effect of the 1 percentage point increase in long-term bond rates of about 75 billion lire (a little more than half the total effect) corresponds to about 1.5 per cent of annual investment. If these quarterly estimates are acceptable, the effects of changes in the cost of credit can not, however, be regarded as insignificant, though they would in themselves be insufficient to explain the modest decline in construction investment in the 1963-64 recession and the much larger decline in 1970-71.

On the whole, the role of the financial variables emerging in the expenditure relationships is not very clear. The impact of interest rate changes on industrial investment appears to be modest, and reservations remain about any firm interpretations of the effects of monetary policy. It must be recalled that the relationships do not allow for any feed-back from real demand to the financial variables though this aspect of mutual interdependence is bound to be pronounced, particularly when one looks at annual data. From a policy viewpoint it is unfortunate that no direct interpretation of the impact of changes in the main operating target of monetary policy, the monetary base, is possible: the financial variables which do appear in the expenditure functions are generally only under indirect influence, and even the rather modest impact they appear to have can not, therefore, be directly interpreted as an effect of monetary policy. In any case, an assessment of the transmission mechanism in sufficient detail to serve as a basis for judgement of the role of monetary policy in short-run demand management requires more detailed study of the time pattern.

Apart from the relative weakness of the links from financial variables to the main components of private expenditures, the most interesting aspect of the results surveyed is that the impact of monetary policy appears to be transmitted more through interest rates than availability effects. The evidence, surveyed in Part III, of a considerable degree of substitutability among domestic financial assets and liabilities and of close linkages to other financial centres would have made unlikely any finding that particular financial stock variables such as bank loans or new bond issues exert a clear influence on consumption and investment. Any verdict must, of course, remain preliminary; as in other countries changes in the degree of credit availability are not directly observable and they tend to be systematically related to interest rate changes, so that effects attributed to the latter might be due to rationing.

The more general conclusion emerging both from the impressionistic survey of the time series and from the two attempts at constructing an econometric model of the real sector of the Italian economy is that monetary policy cannot be shown to have been the major determinant of observed fluctuations in economic activity. It would, however, be wrong to interpret failure to establish any firm conclusions about the effects of monetary policy— even in view of the very considerable research efforts deployed by the Bank of Italy and others— as evidence that the measures taken have had only very limited effects. Such a conclusion would also be at variance with views widely held by informed observers of the Italian economy. There are many aspects of reality which cannot be reflected in models. One such aspect is the effect of the suddenness and vigour with which the two phases of restraint were introduced, following lenghty periods of expansionary or accommodating policy. These changes of policy undoubtedly had an important impact on business expectations on these two occasions, though the evidence that investment demand was decelerating before the announcement of monetary restraint suggests that other factors were more important in shaping expectations. The evidence does not permit one to draw any conclusions as to what would have happened had these other factors, which may be subsumed under the heading of confidence in economic and political stability, remained constant around the introduction of monetary restraint. There is no doubt that the first phase of restraint reduced investment in 1964-65 below the levels which would otherwise have been attained, and the models with their emphasis on average relationships in the transmission mechanism of monetary policy undoubtedly illustrate this effect, though it is difficult to see how the monetary factors could be seen as the major cause of the investment slump. With the exception of the two phases of restraint, Italian monetary policy has since 1960 been designed mainly to provide a stable financial background for economic growth, and indeed for greater social and political stability, rather than to achieve any "fine tuning" of the economy.

c) THE IMPACT ON ULTIMATE POLICY OBJECTIVES

The preliminary nature of the evidence relating to the working of the real sector of the Italian economy precludes any quantification of the contribution made by monetary policy to the achievement of the domestic policy objectives of high and stable resource utilization and price stability. The most that can be said with some confidence is that the orders of magnitude suggested for the impact of financial variables are small in

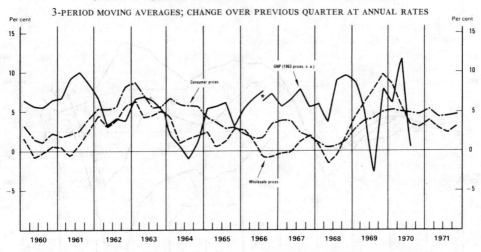

Chart 10. GROSS NATIONAL PRODUCT AND PRICES

3-PERIOD MOVING AVERAGES; CHANGE OVER PREVIOUS QUARTER AT ANNUAL RATES

relation to total real private expenditures, and therefore small also in relation to the rough measures of unutilized resources found in the calculations of a GNP gap. The direct impact of a one percentage point lowering of long-term interest rates appears to have been at most 100 billion lire (pp. 56-57) in the course of a year; this is less than one quarter of a per cent of recent GNP. The evidence, therefore, would be consistent with the view that the slack in the Italian economy could not have been reduced substantially by monetary expansion in the range of policy options which may be considered feasible. Relatively to the excess demand which monetary restraint attempted to eliminate in 1963 and in 1969-70, the effects of monetary policy cannot, however, be considered negligible. It is also possible that the effects were somewhat more important in the two restrictive periods than the average effects for the whole period would indicate.

Greater price stability was another domestic objective of policy, but it may be recalled that the authorities have been concerned about it mainly in two periods: during the price acceleration in 1962-63, and since 1969. In the latter of these two periods, the main concern after the initial tightening of policy tended to shift towards growth and employment. In the early phase of monetary restraint, prices increases slowed down markedly, but prices had begun to decelerate even before the introduction of restraint (Chart 10). In general, there is insufficient knowledge of the relationship between the level of demand pressure in labour and commodity markets and the rate of change in prices to permit any conclusion about the time lags with which changes in monetary policy influence prices, and the total strength of this influence.

It is on the balance of payments that the appearance of policy effects is most clear (Chart 11). The current balance was back in surplus in early 1964, within six months of the tightening of policy. Only a small part of this sudden swing can be attributed to the direct and indirect effects

Chart 11.   BALANCE OF PAYMENTS
4-QUARTER MOVING AVERAGES

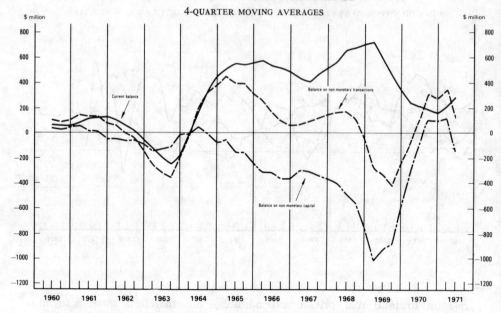

of policy; exports surged ahead to meet strong foreign demand in Western Europe and North America, while imports were sluggish in mirroring the decline in domestic demand, notably investment.   Since 1964 the current account surplus has been remarkably stable and, given the modest impact of monetary policy on domestic demand, there was only limited scope for influencing its size.   The capital account reverted to deficit, following some recovery during the 1963-64 phase of restraint, and offset part of the current surplus, until the sharp worsening in 1968-69 sent the overall balance on non-monetary transactions into deficit.   The wish of the Italian monetary authorities to continue the policy of stable interest rates during this phase, when rates elsewhere were rising sharply, was clearly a major factor behind the outflow.   Their ability to check the flow was brought strongly into evidence when policy was changed in several ways around the middle of the year; the outflow of resident funds was reduced, particularly the export of bank notes, while the inflow of non-resident funds was stepped up, mainly by public sector borrowing encouraged by the monetary authorities.   Since then, the Italian balance of payments has reverted to the pattern familiar from the mid-1960s with a sizeable current surplus partly offset by capital outflows.   While this is obviously not an equilibrium situation in any basic sense, it is difficult to see how a more vigorous application of monetary policy could have brought about such an equilibrium.

V

CONCLUDING REMARKS

The main problems in managing demand in the Italian economy have been structural rather than cyclical in the period since 1960. The prevailing emphasis in the design of monetary policy has accordingly been to encourage a growth rate of demand more in line with the supply potential; to achieve this aim, liquidity creation has been kept rather high and stable, while interest rates have varied only little up to 1969. Important measures have been undertaken to widen financial markets, notably the bond market which is now very large by international standards.

The attempts to gear monetary policy to steady expansion were, however, interrupted during two periods of rather vigorous restraint in 1963-64 and in 1969-70. In both cases the motivation was provided by an acceleration of costs and prices coinciding with a worsening of the balance of payments. In both cases the balance of payments improved quickly. In the first period, domestic demand weakened rather sharply and prices decelerated; but there is some doubt, both from the speed and the strength of these subsequent developments, whether a major role may be attributed to monetary policy. In particular, the deceleration of investment demand prior to the introduction of monetary restraint suggests that other factors related to the confidence of the business community in the economic and political stability of Italy were more important.

The juxtaposition, in the period studied, of long periods of monetary expansion and short periods of rather vigorous restraint makes an assessment of the response of private expenditures to monetary action particularly hazardous in the case of Italy. The evidence presented relates to an average response of the economy to two rather different kinds of experience: an expansionary policy aimed at longer-run structural objectives, and two periods of restraint; and the evidence may not be particularly representative of either experience. The importance of changes in the economic and social climate in shaping the course of the economy, and the incompleteness of the statistical data available, are additional reasons for caution in drawing conclusions about the impact of monetary policy.

Italian experience, however, appears to be a good illustration of the general proposition that, in an open economy with fixed exchange rates, monetary policy is more effective in achieving the external aim of a balance on non-monetary transactions than in influencing domestic policy objectives. The net movement of non-monetary capital has been closely linked to changes in interest rate differentials between Italy and the Euro-dollar market and to changes in domestic monetary policy; the recovery

61

of the capital account in 1969-70 was a major policy achievement. These experiences suggest that, provided speculation in exchange markets is not important, the Italian authorities are in a position to use changes in the net foreign position of the Bank of Italy and of the commercial banks vis-à-vis non-residents as an instrument to determine changes in official reserves. The ability of the Italian authorities to achieve near equilibrium in non-monetary transactions under these conditions, has been clearly demonstrated in the period under study. This is remarkable in view of the size of the current account surplus since the mid-1960s.

The current account surplus itself appears to have been singularly insensitive to expansionary monetary policies. This was no doubt largely because of the latter's apparently limited impact on the pace of general economic expansion. In designing monetary policy, the authorities had no external/internal dilemma: in an environment of relatively stable nominal interest rates which helped to stabilize the balance on non-monetary transactions, the policy to generate, through domestic sources, rapid growth in the monetary base and broader monetary aggregates was not contradictory to the main domestic policy objective of reducing slack in the Italian economy. In practice, however, the response of private expenditures has been sluggish, although the authorities succeeded in maintaining ample flows of credit in recent years.

Empirical studies, reviewed earlier, suggest that the transmission of monetary policy effects through financial markets has generally worked more through changes in interest rates than through variations in the availability of credit. This may be interpreted as a sign that the degree of substitution between various forms of financing is greater than the apparent institutional rigidities and the obvious differences between bank loans and bonds could lead one to believe. On the other hand, there is evidence of availability effects in both the market for bank loans and the bond market during the restrictive phase in 1970. The general conclusion on the relative importance of interest rate effects, therefore, needs to be modified with respect to the experiences in 1970. More generally, it is possible that the finding mainly of an interest rate effect is due to the predominance of the long expansionary policy phases during 1960-71; had there been more periods of vigorous restraint initiated by rationing of central bank credit, the balance of the conclusion on the transmission mechanism might have needed modification.

Since the mid-1960s the Bank of Italy has used the concept of the monetary base as a framework for the formulation of its policy. Changes in the monetary base are largely determined by changes in the main instruments of monetary policy; and the base, in turn, is linked to the total flow of bank credit through a supply relationship which is unstable in the short run, but rather stable over longer periods (one year or more). However, interest rates play a considerable role in the supply of bank credit, and changes in the base have a sizeable impact on market interest rates. If this impact were firm and predictable, it would make little practical difference whether the authorities formulated their policy in terms of monetary base creation or interest rates. But the link does not appear so firm in Italy, particularly in recent years, as to make the choice of no practical importance, and the relationship will no doubt have to be kept under review regularly in the light of the ever-increasing interaction with monetary conditions elsewhere and of the domestic effects desired. On the one hand, the process of financial integration makes it easier to obtain a sizeable impact on capital flows, but on the other hand it poses narrower constraints on the degree of interest rate variation feasible. The authorities have in the past displayed a pragmatic attitude to this problem, notably during the period of stable bond rates in 1966-69, when a policy aiming more directly at interest rates was pursued.

APPENDICES

Appendix A

MAJOR INSTRUMENTS OF MONETARY POLICY

INTRODUCTION

As described in the body of this paper (Part II), the principal proxi-
mate objective of Italian monetary policy is to control the volume of the
monetary base. Whether the banks will use any additions to the monetary
base (less that part used by the public in the form of expanded currency
holdings) to expand their deposit and lending activity depends on the
demand for credit and, to some extent, on the possible earnings on
"excess" reserves— that portion of the monetary base held by the banks
but not required for compulsory reserves. The allocation between required
reserves and free (or excess) reserves can also, in principle, be affected
by changing the required reserve ratio, or the composition of eligible reserve
assets. Since the reserve requirement is the fulcrum on which the system
operates, it will be described first in this appendix, followed by a description
of the three other major mechanisms through which the authorities seek
to affect the volume (sources) and disposition (utilisation) of the monetary
base.

I. THE SYSTEM OF COMPULSORY RESERVE REQUIREMENTS[1]

a) *General Remarks*

Reserve requirements were introduced originally in 1926 as liquidity
ratios to protect depositors. They have been used since 1947 as a tool
of monetary policy. Changing reserve ratios is a cumbersome instrument, however, because of the complex formulae determining the ratios
applicable to different categories of institutions and deposits and because
of the variety of assets that can be held to satisfy the requirements. Thus
in the postwar period the ratio has been changed across-the-board only
once, in a downward direction, in 1962; modifications in 1964 and in 1965
freed certain types of deposits altogether from cash reserve requirements and
reduced the effective ratios applying to other types of deposits. In late
1970, the Bank of Italy released a portion of the reserves impounded in the
form of cash or Treasury bills by allowing the substitution of an equivalent
amount of specified long-term securities. Other, more frequent, changes in

---

1. See also Francesco Masera, "La Riserva Obbligatoria nel Sistema Istituzionale
Italiano", *Quaderni di Ricerche* N. 8, Rome 1971, and N. Fratianni, "Bank Credit and
Money Supply Processes in an Open Economy: A Model Applicable to Italy", *Metro-
economica* 1972.

the definition of assets that satisfy reserve requirements were intended partly as selective credit devices to channel some of the banks' investments in specific directions, and partly to provide the banks with a yield on a portion of their compulsory reserves more attractive than that paid on cash deposits with the Bank of Italy or on Treasury bills specifically held to satisfy reserve requirements. Unlike those in other major countries (e.g. France, Germany, United States), the Italian banks do receive interest on their reserve deposits. The rate, which is approximately equal to the basic discount rate, was a relatively low 3.75 to 3.88 per cent (as will be explained below) from 1959 to 1970. At present it is 5.50 to 5,82 per cent. The evolution of the volume and composition of compulsory reserves is shown in Chart A, that of the effective average ratios in Chart 1.

b) *Mechanics*

All banks must hold minimum reserves against all deposits of non-bank residents, including public bodies,[1] and the lire deposits of non-residents.[2] However, the ratios and the definition of assets which satisfy the requirements vary according to the type of deposit and of banking institution. Banks have considerable leeway in selecting the date to which reserve requirements apply. For example, to calculate the reserves applying to the month of January, a bank may choose the day with the lowest deposits outstanding between 31st January and 10th February; reserves, whatever the form in which they may be held, must be deposited with the Bank of Italy on 25th February, and held until 25th March. If deposits decline during this period, a corresponding decrease in the cash reserve balance must take place. The Bank of Italy pays a higher rate of interest on required reserve deposits than on free cash deposits.

c) *Commercial banks*

Commercial banks' deposits are subject to progressively higher requirements depending on the ratio of an individual commercial bank's deposit liabilities to its capital plus reserves, with the proviso that the maximum ratio for an individual bank cannot exceed 22.5 per cent.[3] The maximum ratio was 25 per cent from 1947 to 31st January 1962.

Between January 1953 and December 1962, commercial banks could satisfy reserve requirements by any combination of cash deposits[4] or Treasury bills[5] with the Bank of Italy (Chart A). Reserve deposits are remunerated at a yield approximately equal to the basic discount rate. Thus cash deposits with the central bank then yielded 3.75 per cent[6] and

---

1. The central government does not hold any deposits with the banks.
2. Foreign currency deposits are not subject to reserve requirements.
3. Until 31st December 1962 lira deposits of non-residents were subject to a flat 50 per cent reserve requirement; since then they are subject to the same requirement as lira deposits of residents.
4. Vault cash is not counted as an asset satisfying the compulsory reserve ratio.
5. Since November 1962 all Treasury bills in Italy have been of one year maturity.
6. 3.5 per cent basic discount rate plus 0.25 per cent premium.

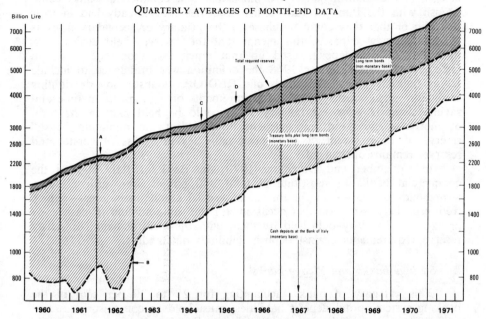

Chart A. BANKING SYSTEM'S REQUIRED RESERVES

QUARTERLY AVERAGES OF MONTH-END DATA

A. 31 Jan. 1962: Maximum ratio reduced from 25 to 22.5 per cent for commercial banks.

B. 1 Dec. 1962: Minimum "cash deposit" requirement introduced for commercial banks.

C. 23 Oct. 1964: Savings banks allowed to hold their reserves entirely in the form of specified long-term bonds.

D. 30 Sep. 1965: Commercial banks allowed to hold, partly in the form of specified long-term bonds, reserves against increments in savings deposits.

Treasury bills 3.88 per cent[1]. Since November 1962 the Treasury bills to be used for required reserves have had to be purchased directly from the Treasury.

Effective 1st December 1962 commercial banks were required to maintain a minimum cash (deposit) balance with the Central bank equal to 10 per cent of the excess of deposit liabilities over capital plus reserves. The remainder of the requirement could still be satisfied in the form of cash deposits of Treasury bills. In October 1970 the yields were raised to 5.5 per cent for deposits and 5.82 per cent for Treasury bills.

After 30th September 1965, reserves against increments in time and savings deposits of commercial banks could be satisfied with a wide range of long-term securities, including real estate (cartelle fondiarie) and agricultural land improvement bonds (cartelle agrarie di miglioramento), subject

---

1. Treasury bills were sold at a discount of 3.5 per cent (equal to the basic discount rate) yielding an effective return of 3.63 per cent. In addition, until May 1969, banks were paid a premium of 0.25 per cent.

to the proviso that a minimum of 10 per cent of total deposits be held in cash at the Central bank. To the extent that commercial banks could deposit with the Bank of Italy either securities they already had in their portfolio or that they could purchase in the primary or secondary markets by creating new deposits, this meant that the reserves held against new time and savings deposits used up that much less monetary base. In October 1967 and January 1968 the definition was broadened to include school building bonds and bonds of CREDIOP, an institution distributing credit for public works. Reserve requirements on increments in time and savings deposits after 1st January 1970 could be held only in the form of mortgage and land improvement bonds. But the minimum "cash" reserve of 10 per cent of all deposit liabilities in excess of capital and reserves remains unchanged.

In November and December 1970, the Bank of Italy allowed the commercial banks to substitute in total 260 billion lire worth of long-term bonds of IMI— one of the major special credit institutions— which were especially issued on that occasion, for the same amount of cash and/or expiring Treasury bills held by them with the Central bank, to satisfy reserve requirements against deposit liabilities outstanding.

d) *Savings banks and Pledge banks*[1]

This category of banks, accounting for 25 to 30 per cent of the banking system's total deposit liabilities, must hold as compulsory reserves only 20 per cent of the increments in deposits after 1st September 1958. Their reserves take the form of deposits with ICCRI (the central credit institution of the savings banks, which coordinates their activity and acts as a clearing house for financial information and assistance). Until September 1964, ICCRI could reinvest freely in the bond market up to 50 per cent of the reserves deposited with it (with no use of monetary base by the banking system) but had to redeposit the remaining 50 per cent with the Bank of Italy in the form of cash or Treasury bills (with a consequent use of monetary base). Since October 1964, ICCRI is no longer required to hold Treasury bills or deposits with the Bank of Italy. It can satisfy its reserve requirements by holding designated long-term securities. Thus, at present, no monetary base is absorbed by the required reserves of the savings and pledge banks.[2]

e) *Rural and Handicraft banks*

These banks (accounting for a very small proportion of the banking system's total deposit liabilities) are subject to either 10 or 20 per cent reserve requirements depending on whether they are incorporated as joint stock companies with unlimited or limited liability. Their requirements are also satisfied by holding a combination of designated long-term securities, and therefore do not absorb any monetary base.[2]

---

1. Pledge banks (Monti di Credito su Pegno di Prima Categoria) were originally pawn offices established as philanthropic foundations. Over the years, their activity has grown to encompass a wide range of commercial banking functions.
2. But their deposits are included in calculating the ratios shown in Chart 5. Unlike commercial banks, neither savings banks, nor ICCRI, nor Rural and Handicraft Banks were ever subject to the 10 per cent minimum cash deposit with the Bank of Italy.

II. THE MANAGEMENT OF THE BANKS' FOREIGN POSITION

The regulation of the banks' net foreign position[1] is used primarily as a device to assist in financing balance of payments surpluses (or deficits) and thus to prevent an excessive accumulation (or decline) in official foreign reserves. But it is also used to influence the amount of liquid foreign assets held by the banks that can be freely repatriated, and which thus constitute part of the monetary base. The mechanics of the system are summarised in the following paragraphs; a sample classification of Italian banks' accounts vis-à-vis non-residents in shown in Table A.

TABLE A. CLASSIFICATION OF ITALIAN BANKS' ACCOUNTS
VIS-A-VIS NON-RESIDENTS

LEVELS OUTSTANDING ON 30TH JUNE 1969; BILLION LIRE EQUIVALENT

I. ASSETS	*3,599*
A. *Liquid*	517
(Convertible foreign exchange and coin held in vault; sight deposits with foreign correspondents; discounted foreign trade bills in the process of collection; Treasury bills of foreign governments, bankers' acceptances and other debt instruments of very short maturity).	
of which:	
1. Freely repatriable	114
2. Tied as a consequence of prevailing Bank of Italy directives, regarding overall net position	403
B. *Non-liquid*	3,082
(Convertible foreign exchange and lire loans to non-resident banks and non-banks; certificates of deposit, Treasury bills of foreign governments, Euro-currency deposits, and other foreign debt instruments of longer maturity than "liquid assets"; and an insignificant amount of assets in non-convertible currencies).	
II. LIABILITIES	*3,481*
(Non-resident bank and non-bank convertible foreign exchange and lire deposits of different maturities; loans).	
III. NET POSITION VIS-A-VIS NON-RESIDENTS (I — II)	*+ 118*

The Bank of Italy gives overall instructions regarding the banks' net foreign position— e.g. complete freedom to hold any position, positive or negative; a ceiling on net indebtedness; a balanced position *only;* any net positive position.[2] Within this framework, the banks are free to decide the amount and the form of *gross* assets and *gross* liabilities they wish to hold. Thus, the quantity of freely repatriable *liquid assets* held by the banks is the result of the Bank of Italy's overall instructions, and the banks' decisions regarding the amount of liquid assets they wish to hold, as will be shown in examples below.[3]

---

1. "Net foreign position" is defined as the position vis-à-vis non-residents in all currencies.
2. Other combinations are possible, but only the ones mentioned have, in fact, been used.
3. See also Fratianni, *op. cit.*

The bulk of the banks' foreign assets is invested in non-liquid form, but a certain amount of their assets is also kept in liquid form (see Table A for definitions):

  i)   as working reserves against foreign liabilities;
  ii) as a cushion of potential liquidity for possible repatriation to meet sudden domestic liquidity drains.

A bank may decide, of its own choice, not to hold any foreign asset in a liquid form. In this case, no liquid assets (monetary base) would exist as a result of the banks' foreign operations. But even if a bank chose to hold part or all of its foreign assets in liquid form, the Bank of Italy's overall instructions could in effect lock up all or a portion of these assets, which in the Italian statistics would then be classified as "tied" liquid assets (see Table A), as will be shown in the example below. In that case banks may choose to transform these locked-in liquid assets into higher yielding non-liquid assets. But, in practice, they do not always seem to do so, perhaps because they wish to hold liquid foreign assets to meet sudden withdrawals of foreign liabilities. Thus the impact on creation of monetary base of the management of foreign exchange balances is the result of normal banking practice combined with Bank of Italy instructions.[1] The following paragraphs illustrate the mechanics of the system under the different Bank of Italy overall instructions which have prevailed since 1962.

Case A. The Bank of Italy permits banks to hold any net position they wish:

  — Liquid foreign assets are *all* repatriable. This was the case between November 1962 and September 1963.

Case B. The Bank of Italy sets a maximum limit on the net external indebtedness of each individual bank:

  — If a bank is at the maximum ceiling of indebtedness, that bank has no repatriable liquid assets, because any reduction of its assets would cause its net debtor position to exceed the ceiling. This was generally the case from October to December 1963.
  — If an individual bank's overall foreign indebtedness is below the ceiling, it can repatriate liquid assets until by doing so it reaches the upper limit of net indebtedness. This was generally the case from January 1964 to October 1965.

Case C. The Bank of Italy instructs banks to maintain *at least* a net balanced position, i.e. an individual bank's gross foreign assets must be equal to, or greater than, its gross liabilities:

  — If a bank has a balanced position, all the liquid assets it holds are frozen; any repatriation would make its overall net position negative.
  — If a bank's net positive position is equal to or greater than its liquid assets, all its liquid assets are repatriable; repatriation of all its liquid assets would not make the overall balance negative.

---

1. It seems questionable whether the changes in the monetary base resulting from Bank of Italy instructions have implications for the supply of bank credit similar to those arising from other sources of change in the base, e.g. open market operations.

— If a bank has a net positive position smaller than its liquid assets, it can repatriate liquid assets only up to an amount equal to its net positive position. Repatriation of a larger amount of liquid assets would make the overall net position negative.

— If a bank had a net negative position when the regulation went into effect, il would have to purchase foreign exchange from the Central bank in order either to reduce its gross foreign liabilities or to increase its gross assets, until the two were equal.

All the alternatives described seem to have occurred between November 1965 and March 1969.

Case D. The Bank of Italy instructs banks having a positive net foreign position to bring it into equilibrium and to maintain thereafter *only* a net balanced position; i.e. banks must either reduce their *gross* assets or increase their *gross* liabilities until the two are brought into balance, but cannot move into a net negative position:

— If a bank chose to reduce its gross assets, it could do so only to the extent they were liquid. If its liquid assets at the time the directive was issued were at least as large as the net position to be eliminated, there would have been no change in the monetary base, since the liquid assets that were to be repatriated were already counted as part of the monetary base. If its liquid assets were smaller than the net position it had to eliminate, it could meet the requirement either by liquefying some of its foreign assets, or by increasing its foreign liabilities; in either case, the final outcome would be a sale of foreign exchange to the Central bank, and the monetary base would thereby be increased.[1] This was the case between March and June 1969, and both alternatives described seem to have taken place.

— Once equilibrium has been reached, all liquid assets are frozen; any repatriation of these assets would make a bank's net overall position negative. This is the case from the end-June 1969 to the end of the period under review.

One final point to bear in mind is that the Bank of Italy never tells the banks to maintain a *specified* net long position. It may tell the banks to maintain no less than, say, a balanced position. But to induce them to place funds abroad, if they would not do so under the influence of purely market forces, the Bank of Italy supplements its directives with a system of profit incentives, supplying the banks with favourable forward cover through swap transactions.

III. THE DISCOUNT MECHANISM

a) *Credit to the banking system*

In Italy the banking system does not have automatic access to central bank credit. The acceptance of each credit application is subject to the discretion of the Bank of Italy, which makes its decision on the basis of the situation with respect to the creation of monetary base, general liquidity

---

1. Actually, in the *first* of these two alternatives, the monetary base would increase when the foreign asset was liquefied, rather than when it was repatriated.

conditions of the market, and the position of the applicant bank. Moreover, for eleven years the emphasis was on controlling the availability rather than the cost of central bank credit. From 1958 to 1969 the basic discount rate remained unchanged at 3.5 per cent and no penalty rate was charged for frequent or exceptional borrowing. In 1969, however, the pressure of rising interest rates abroad, and the large capital outflows experienced by Italy, induced the monetary authorities to increase the cost as well as to reduce the availability of central bank credit. In March 1969 penalty rates were introduced on borrowing in excess of certain limits, and subsequently the basic discount rate was increased, as will be reviewed below.

i) *Types of accommodation*

Bank of Italy credit takes mainly the form of *advances on collateral*. These are made on the basis of confirmed lines of credit, which the Bank opens in favour of the banking system against securities deposited with it. The upper limit of these credit lines generally varies between 3 and 5 per cent of the borrowing bank's total deposit liabilities. The paper eligible as collateral consists mostly of government securities, mortgage bonds and bonds of special credit institutions and nationalised enterprises. The commercial banks are not expected to draw the credit at once and remain fully indebted for the duration of that period; rather it is expected that there will be a continuous flow of drawings and repayments. The difference between the total approved line of credit and the balance actually drawn is included in the banks' excess reserves (liquid assets) and in the monetary base.

In 1967, the Bank of Italy introduced a supplement to the credit instrument noted above, namely *advances on collateral with a fixed maturity* of 8, 15, or 22 days, which must be drawn in full when granted. Beginning in March 1969, a penalty rate has been applied to these advances (see below).

The second major type of accommodation consists in the *rediscounting* of commercial paper. To be eligible, paper must have no more than four months to maturity at the time of discounting.[1]

Collateral advances as well as rediscounts are available as a privilege subject to the discretion of the Bank of Italy. Confirmed collateral loan lines come up for review every four months, and the Bank of Italy can, in principle, reduce the lines at that time. But, in practice, the adjustments have always been upward, in relation to the individual bank's growth of deposit activity.[2] There is no quota or ceiling for rediscounts and fixed term advances. Thus, the amount granted is fully within the discretion of

---

1. Another type of central bank accommodation consists of the rediscounting of Storage Agency Bills (Ammassi Obbligatori), i.e. bills issued until 1964 to finance the government's farm price support programme (particularly the price of wheat). These bills, which are first discounted with the banks, are automatically eligible for rediscounting at the Bank of Italy, and are for the most part passed on to the latter. In this instance, the Bank of Italy acts as agent for the government and in fact the Bank treats such discounts as credit to the Treasury rather than to the banking system. Banks include in their liquid assets (excess reserves) any of these bills they still hold in their portfolios; they are, therefore, counted as part of the monetary base.
2. See first paragraph above.

the Bank of Italy at the moment of extension of the credit, and no monetary base is created until that time.

The evolution of the volume and composition of Bank of Italy credit to the banking system is shown in Chart B. It will be noticed that, except in periods of tightening, advances on collateral loan lines form the most important part of central bank credit. Apart from the influence of the Central bank on the form in which it grants credit, there are other reasons why, normally, the banks prefer to draw on their collateral loan line, rather than resorting to rediscounting and, since 1967, to fixed term advances. First of all, even at identical basic rediscount or loan rates, borrowing under the collateral loan line could result in lower interest costs than the alternative forms of borrowing. This is because interest is charged only on outstanding debtor balances and banks have the option of repaying or reducing their indebtedness at any time; on fixed term advances and rediscounts, on the other hand, interest has to be paid for the full life of the loan, there being no provision for advance repayment. Also, on rediscounts, the interest is deducted in advance, thereby raising the real effective rate. Moreover, when the banks rediscount paper, the Bank of Italy's signature and seal appears on it, and, as a normal commercial practice, the banks do not wish their customers to see that their paper has been sold to the Central bank.

ii) *Cost of central bank credit*

As noted, the cost of borrowing (in any form) at the Bank of Italy remained unchanged at 3.5 per cent from 1958 to 1969. During that period the emphasis was on rationing the availability of central bank credit. Moreover, the capital outflows that occurred during that period were not mainly induced, at least until late in the period, by interest rate differentials. Another, less important, reason why frequent changes in the discount rate were avoided has been explained by the Bank of Italy as follows:[1] traditionally the Central bank pays interest on the reserve balances of the commercial banks. Therefore, any change in the discount rate would be, eventually, followed by a corresponding change in the interest paid on required reserves.[2]

Thus, a reduction in the discount rate, with a corresponding reduction in the interest paid on banks' reserves, might have a perverse effect on the cost and availability of commercial bank loans. Some 10 to 15 per cent (using 1971 figures, see Chart 1) of the banks' assets would earn interest at the reduced rate, while only a negligible amount of funds— those borrowed from the Central bank— would be supplied at a lower cost. Thus, in order to maintain their earnings, banks would have to increase their lending rates. On the other hand, if the banks tried to offset their income loss by reducing the rates they pay on deposits, the flow of deposits into the banks might shrink, diminishing the volume of funds available for lending.

---

1. BIS, *Some Questions Relating to the Structure of Interest Rates,* July 1968, page 19.
2. In fact, the June 1958 reduction of the basic discount rate from 4 to 3.5 per cent was accompanied on the same day by a reduction from 4.25 to 3.75 per cent on the rate paid on compulsory reserves. The discount rate increases of 1969-1970, which brought the rate to 5.5 per cent in March 1970, were followed in October by an increase to 5.5 per cent in the interest paid on banks' compulsory reserves.

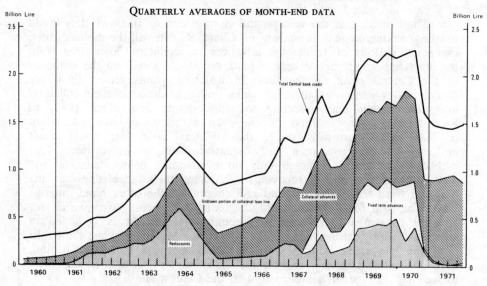

Chart B. BANK OF ITALY CREDIT TO BANKING SYSTEM
QUARTERLY AVERAGES OF MONTH-END DATA

However, measures adopted since March 1969, under the pressure of developments in international money and capital markets, have resulted in a system which relates the cost of the credit extended by the Central bank to the amount and frequency of financing granted to an individual bank. In March 1969, penalty rates were established for *fixed term advances* to banks which utilise this form of financing more than once in any six month period. The penalty is half of a percentage point above the basic discount rate for the second transaction, one percentage point for the third, and one and a half percentage points for subsequent ones. In July 1969 a 1.5 percentage point surcharge over the basic rate was established on *ordinary rediscount operations* whenever, during the preceding calendar semester, the applicant bank had, on the average, outstanding rediscounts exceeding five per cent of its required reserve assets as of the middle of that period. Finally price and balance of payments trends led the Bank of Italy to raise the basic discount rate from 3.5 to 4.0 per cent in August 1969 and to 5.5 per cent in May 1970.

From 1954 until the end of 1969 the discount rate was also supposed to affect the banks' lending rates. During that period, minimum lending rates and maximum deposit rates were set by the commercial banks under a voluntary agreement; minimum lending rates were tied to the discount rate. The agreement which was renewed annually, was never strictly observed. Interest rates higher than those stipulated in the agreement were paid on large deposits; and when Euro-dollar rates were below the minimum domestic lending rates, the Italian banks, to meet competition of foreign banks, kept rates on foreign currency loans to their prime customers below the rates on lira loans. In December 1969 the cartel was abandoned. In September 1970 a new cartel was formed, setting maximum deposit rates.

76

b) *Credit to non-bank borrowers*

In principle, special credit institutions have no access to the Bank of Italy's discount window. But occasionally the Bank extends them credit on a limited scale, to relieve temporary pressures. The Bank may also, at its discretion, make advances to private individuals against approved collateral. In practice, the Bank refrains from making such loans, even though it retains the legal authority to do so under emergency circumstances. The Bank does not extend credit to provincial and municipal governments. Credit to the central government is discussed in Section I of the main text (page 12).

IV. OPEN MARKET OPERATIONS

a) *General remarks*

Open market operations affecting monetary base have acquired relative significance in Italy only since 1966, as shown in Table B. The Bank of Italy is limited by law to open market operations in government or government-guaranteed securities. Until April 1969 such operations could take place only in long term securities. Since then operations in Treasury bills are also possible; but so far they have been virtually nil.

Open market policy in Italy is not used primarily to affect bank reserves or liquidity, although they do, of course, affect bank liquidity (and the monetary base), other things remaining equal. Rather, the primary purpose of these operations seems to be to lend support to the government securities market and to stabilise or to smooth out fluctuations in interest rates.

TABLE B. BANK OF ITALY'S SECURITY PORTFOLIO[1]
CHANGES IN BILLION OF LIRE

Years	Government or government-guaranteed securites			Other securities	Total
	Purchased at issue[2]	Open market operations	Total		
1958	15.4	−5.8	9.6	5.6	15.2
1959	13.2	12.6	25.8	2.0	27.8
1960	0.7	11.6	12.3	5.3	17.6
1961	18.8	16.5	35.3	5.8	41.1
1962	14.2	12.9	27.1	6.0	33.1
1963	−1.3	−7.5	−8.8	5.5	−3.3
1964	158.4	10.0	168.4	10.1	178.5
1965	60.6	−9.0	51.6	—	51.6
1966	436.9	−239.4	197.5	1.9	199.4
1967	475.4	−306.4	169.0	−1.1	167.9
1968	643.0	−423.7	219.3	—	219.3
1969	1,229.8	267.8	1,497.6	—	1,497.6
1970	1,098.4	−172.2	926.2	—	926,2
1971	1,248.2	−145.3	1,102.9	—	1,102.9

1. Excluding Storage Agency bills, and, until 1968, ordinary Treasury bills.
2. Net of retirements.

Institutional factors, especially the non-existence of a short-term money market, account for the relatively modest rate of open market operations. There are several reasons for this lack. One is that Italian banks pay competitive interest rates on demand as well as on time deposits. Another is that a large proportion of bank credit in Italy is extended in the form of overdrafts; therefore, when bank customers have excess cash, they will often use it to reduce their overdrafts. A third reason is the lack of suitable short-term negotiable debt instruments. The government security of shortest maturity is the one-year Treasury bill, and short-term marketable obligations of business enterprises (commercial paper) are almost unknown. Most Treasury bills are held by banks to satisfy compulsory reserve requirements. These have to be held to maturity, but some exceptions have been made since January 1971. From 1962 until April 1969 the Treasury also sold "free" Treasury bills— i.e. bills that could not be used to satisfy reserve requirements— at interest rates close to the official discount rate. But since the Bank of Italy was committed to buying back these bills at no loss of interest, they were in effect as liquid as cash (and were counted as part of the monetary base). In April 1969, the Bank of Italy stopped purchasing such bills and stated that henceforth it would discount them at its own discretion or buy them in open market operations at its own initiative and at competitive interest rates. At the same time the Treasury started making new issues of "free" Treasury bills at interest rates more closely reflecting comparable rates in international markets. So far there have been virtually no purchases of such bills by the banks or the public generally.

b) *Operations in long-term securities*

Open market purchases of long-term securities have grown in recent years, apparently as a concomitant of the interest rate stabilisation policy pursued by the Bank of Italy after the middle of 1966. The amount of medium and long-term indebtedness of the Treasury has nearly trebled since 1964, and at the end of 1969 exceeded 9,500 billion lire.[1] This enlargement has created problems of timing in the emission of new bonds and the redemption of maturing bonds. Thus, from time to time the Central bank has been impelled to absorb parts of the new issues, releasing them to the market later at more favourable times. On rare occasions, public debt operations by the Treasury have also served as a tool of monetary policy. For instances, the Treasury has borrowed in advance of its requirements in order to absorb liquidity; and it has redeemed maturing issues rather than refund them in order to create liquidity.

---

1. For comparison, total tax receipts in 1969 were slightly below 9,000 billion lire, and the ratio to GNP of medium and long-term Treasury indebtedness in that year was 18 per cent.

Appendix B

SELECTED CHRONOLOGY OF MONETARY
MEASURES, 1962-71

1962

JANUARY
Reserve requirements. Required reserves of commercial and savings banks reduced from 25 to 22.5 per cent of deposits, freeing 190 billion lire of reserves, equal to about 2.3 per cent of monetary base outstanding on 31st December 1961.

NOVEMBER
Banks' foreign position. Obligation to maintain no less than a net balanced position in foreign exchange vis-à-vis non-residents abolished, leaving banks free of control on net foreign position in either foreign currency or lire.

1963

OCTOBER
Banks' foreign position. Maximum net debtor position vis-à-vis non-residents frozen at end-September level (840 billion lire) to prevent further inflows of bank capital with consequent additions to monetary base.

1964

JANUARY
Banks' foreign position. Maximum net debtor position vis-à-vis non-residents frozen at lower of end-November or end-December level, reducing ceiling of net indebtedness to 784 billion lire.

FEBRUARY
Hire purchase regulations. Proposal submitted to Parliament for minimum down payment and maximum term on instalment purchases.

JULY
Banks' foreign position. Maximum net debtor position vis-à-vis non-residents frozen at lower of 15th or 30th June position, reducing ceiling on net indebtedness from about 780 to 570 billion lire.

SEPTEMBER
Hire purchase regulations. Law enacted, prescribing minimum down payment of 25 per cent and maximum repayment period or 24 months on wide range of durables, including private automobiles.

OCTOBER
Reserve requirements. Savings banks in effect relieved from holding reserves in the form of cash or Treasury

79

bills, and permitted to hold certain types of long-term securities instead. Primarily designed as a selective credit device, measure also frees a small amount of monetary base.

DECEMBER   *Hire purchase regulations.* Motorcycles and television sets freed from restrictions, because of a sharp drop in sales.

1965

MARCH   *Hire purchase regulations.* Remaining regulations suspended until 31st December 1966.

SEPTEMBER   *Reserve requirements.* Commercial banks partially relieved from holding reserves in the form of cash or Treasury bills against increments in time and savings deposits after 30th September 1965; exempted portion may be held in the form of long-term real estate and land improvement bonds that the banks can acquire by creating deposits. Measure achieves the dual aim of channelling credit in the desired direction and reducing the effective ratio of compulsory reserves held in the form of monetary base.

NOVEMBER   *Banks' foreign position.* To encourage bank capital outflow and help finance balance of payments surplus on non-monetary transactions, banks forbidden to hold negative net position vis-à-vis non-residents.

1967

OCTOBER   *Reserve requirements.* School-building bonds added to list of long-term bonds eligible to be held as reserves (see measures of October 1964 and September 1965). The measure is designed *only* as a selective credit device with no effect on bank liquidity or monetary base.

1968

JANUARY   *Reserve requirements.* Bonds of CREDIOP, an institution distributing credit for public works, added to eligible list of long-term bonds which can be held as reserve assets; reason and effect are the same as October 1967 measure.

1969

MARCH   *Banks' foreign position.* To stop outflow of bank funds and partly to offset outflow of non-bank capital, banks instructed to reduce net position vis-à-vis non-residents (500 billion lire equivalent) to zero by 30th June, 1969 and to maintain balanced position thereafter.

Penalty rate. To help reduce differential between Italian interest rates and higher foreign rates, Bank of Italy's

80

fixed term advances against collateral subjected to penalty rate of up to 1.5 percentage points above basic discount rate (3.5 per cent at the time), depending on frequency with which banks utilise this form or financing in any six month period.

APRIL
Banks' foreign operations. Suspension of general authorisation allowing banks to participate in consortia for the taking-over and placing of foreign security issues and limitation of foreign investment fund operations in Italy. *Treasury bill rate.* Auction rate for "free" Treasury bills allowed to rise.

JUNE
Penalty rate. Penalty rate of up to 1.5 per cent over basic discount rate extended to ordinary rediscounting in excess of certain norms.

AUGUST
Basic discount rate. Increased from 3.5 to 4 per cent.

1970

FEBRUARY
Leads and lags. Terms for import and export payments shortened.
Repatriation of bank notes. Presentation to the Bank of Italy in Rome for conversion compulsory.

MARCH
Basic discount rate. Increased from 4 to 5.5 per cent.

1971

JANUARY
Rate of advances against collateral. Reduced from 5.5 to 5 per cent. Penalty rates (see 1969 March and June) remained unchanged.

APRIL
Basic discount rate. Reduced from 5.5 to 5 per cent in the wake of bank rate reductions of other countries.

OCTOBER
Basic discount rate and rate of advances against collateral. Reduced respectively from 5 to 4.5 per cent and from 5 to 4 per cent again in the wake of similar reductions elsewhere in Europe.

DATA ANNEX

	1961	1962	1963
1. *Uses of funds, total (2 + 3)*	*6,162*	*7,150*	*7,807*
2. Investment	*5,333*	*6,060*	*6,938*
3. Financial assets	*829*	*1,090*	*869*
i) Currency and deposits	829	1,090	869
ii) Securities[1]	—	—	—
iii) Short-term loans	—	—	—
iv) Medium and long-term loans	—	—	—
v) Other identified assets	—	—	—
4. *Sources of funds, total (5 + 6)*	*6,147*	*7,186*	*7,734*
5. Internal funds...	*2,841*	*2,903*	*3,050*
6. External funds	*3,306*	*4,283*	*4,684*
i) Securities[1]	771	1,010	1,010
ii) Short-term loans	1,416	1,851	1,935
iii) Medium and long-term loans	1,119	1,422	1,739
7. Statistical discrepancy (1—4)	15	–36	73

1. Bonds, shares and short-term securities.
2. Includes small amounts of other identified liabilities.

Source: Bank of Italy, *Annual Reports.*

	1961	1962	1963
1. *Uses of funds, total (1 = 2)*	*2,828*	*3,079*	*3,167*
2. Financial assets	*2,828*	*3,079*	*3,167*
i) Currency and deposits	1,355	1,621	1,574
ii) Securities[2]...	1,070	984	984
iii) Other identified assets	403	474	609
3. *Sources of funds, total (4 + 5)*	*2,827*	*3,329*	*3,521*
4. Savings and net transfers	*2,827*	*3,329*	*3,521*
5. Financial liabilities	—	—	—
i) Short-term loans	—	—	—
ii) Medium and long-term loans	—	—	—
6. Statistical discrepancy (1—3)	1	–250	–354

1. Excluding housing, which is included in the enterprise sector.
2. Bonds, shares, and short-term securities.

Source: Bank of Italy, *Annual Reports.*

1964	1965	1966	1967	1968	1969	1970	1971
7,976	8,180	8,907	9,806	10,045	11,945	13,764	14,267
5,657	6,276	6,656	7,820	8,043	9,626	11,242	10,583
1,319	1,904	2,251	1,986	2,002	2,319	2,522	3,684
725	1,618	1,558	1,653	1,459	1,599	1,651	2,448
528	262	366	255	284	349	432	638
—	—	158	−49	226	246	357	523
30	16	130	78	−12	79	40	18
36	8	39	49	45	46	42	57
5,866	6,826	7,904	8,984	9,699	12,202	12,307	13,899
3,366	4,165	4,595	5,001	5,653	6,907	6,726	6,498
2,500	2,661	3,309	3,983	4,046	5,295	5,581	7,401
1,114	1,238	791	870	1,282	1,329	1,174	1,951
51	606	1,606	1,813	1,244	2,436	2,275	1,868
1,335	817	912	1,300	1,520	1,530[2]	2,132[2]	3,582[2]
2,110	1,354	1,003	822	346	−257	1,457	368

USEHOLD SECTOR[1]

IRE

1964	1965	1966	1967	1968	1969	1970	1971
1,948	3,515	4,474	4,986	5,525	6,488	7,096	9,290
1,948	3,515	4,474	4,986	5,525	6,488	7,096	9,290
1,247	2,122	2,447	2,807	2,971	3,192	4,820	6,349
5	764	1,262	1,229	1,383	1,383	1,153	1,826
696	629	765	950	1,171	1,913	1,123	1,115
3,829	4,886	5,071	4,956	5,761	6,804	7,612	9,730
3,703	4,649	4,695	4,511	5,226	6,384	6,955	9,152
126	237	376	445	535	420	657	578
−5	48	83	120	175	104	141	138
131	189	293	325	360	316	516	440
−1,881	−1,371	−597	30	−236	−316	−516	−440

	1961	1962	19
1. Uses of funds, total (2 + 3)	710	757	8.
2. Investment	710	757	8
3. Financial assets	—	—	—
i) Currency and deposits	—	—	—
ii) Securities[1]	—	—	—
iii) Short-term loans	—	—	—
iv) Medium and long-term loans	—	—	—
v) Other identified assets	—	—	—
4. Sources of funds, total (5 + 6)	1,030	1,033	1,2:
5. Savings and net transfers	671	734	7:
6. Financial liabilities	359	299	49
i) Currency and deposits	—	—	
ii) Securities[1]	164	74	7
iii) Short-term loans	195	225	42
iv) Medium and long-term loans	—	—	
v) Other identified liabilities	—	—	—
7. Statistical discrepancy (1—4)	−320	−276	−39

1. Bonds, shares, and short-term securities.
Source: Bank of Italy, *Annual Reports.*

	1960	1961	1962	196
1. Net new security issues purchased by non-bank public and non-bank financial intermediaries[1]	1,122	1,178	1,233	1,15
of which: *i)* Private sector issues...........	935	1,123	1,207	1,17
ii) Government issues............	187	55	26	−1
2. Domestic credit (including acquisition of net new security issues) by the banking system including the Bank of Italy	1,549	1,674	2,965	3,28
of which: *i)* To private sector	1,548	1,571	2,447	2,57
ii) To government	1	103	518	70
3. Total (1 + 2)..............................	2,671	2,852	4,198	4,44
of which percentage share:				
i) To private sector	93	94	87	8
ii) To government	7	6	13	1
iii) Extended by non-banks	42	41	29	2
iv) Extended by banks	58	59	71	7
4. Total as percentage of GNP	12	12	15	1

1. Total net new security issues less acquisitions by the banking system, including the Bank of Italy (line 15 minus lines 11 and 12 of Table A5).
NOTE Private sector includes state-owned organisations such as ENEL, ENI, IRI; special credit institutions; and provinces and municipalities. government includes only central government.
Source: Bank of Italy, *Annual Reports.*

964	1965	1966	1967	1968	1969	1970	1971
,498	1,341	928	2,341	2,828	3,481	2,758	4,473
978	939	1,014	963	1,187	1,509	1,724	1,887
520	402	−86	1,378	1,641	1,972	1,034	2,586
34	116	−549	−92	262	349	−112	760
291	232	104	159	434	272	261	817
—	—	−473	570	80	627	−2	−22
143	145	837	736	868	723	889	1,031
52	−91	−5	5	−3	1	−2	0
,960	1,870	1,788	3,060	3,929	2,830	4,195	4,431
954	−219	−298	270	22	−679	−550	−2,365
,006	2,089	2,086	2,790	3,907	3,509	4,745	6,796
−367	4	59	371	587	855	222	1,026
412	735	1,713	1,020	1,519	1,673	954	3,610
135	383	−826	319	629	−62	2,182	368
619	776	866	794	881	717	1,052	1,440
207	191	274	286	291	326	335	352
−462	−529	−860	−719	−1,101	651	−1,437	42

1964	1965	1966	1967	1968	1969	1970	1971
,395	1,209	1,769	1,643	1,806	1,665	1,774	2,703
,333	1,001	1,113	1,104	1,579	1,494	1,714	2,645
62	208	656	539	227	171	60	58
,483	2,715	3,474	3,669	4,449	5,500	6,664	7,883
917	1,670	2,665	3,556	2,904	4,289	4,138	4,430
566	1,045	809	113	1,545	1,211	2,526	3,453
2,878	3,924	5,243	5,312	6,255	7,165	8,438	10,586
78	68	72	88	72	81	69	67
22	32	28	12	28	19	31	33
48	31	34	31	29	23	21	26
52	69	66	69	71	77	79	74
8	11	13	12	13	14	14	14

	1960	1961	1962	196
Net new issues				
A. Bonds:				
1. Government[1]	143	136	33	−9
2. Public enterprises[2]	99	144	100	35
3. Special credit institutions	412	513	724	7.
4. Private enterprises	196	126	206	4
5. Rest of the world	—	15	30	2
6. Total	850	934	1,093	1,10
B. Shares:				
7. Public enterprises[2]	..	78	186	
8. Private enterprises	..	406	491	37
9. Financial institutions	..	31	39	2
10. Total	496	515	716	39
C. Total net issues (6 + 10)	1,346	1,449	1,809	1,49
Corporate shares in per cent of total	37	36	40	2
Securities acquired by:				
11. Bank of Italy	17	41	54	1
12. Banks	207	230	522	32
13. Non-bank financial institutions[3]	80	107	249	42
14. Non-financial public[4]	1,042	1,070	984	73
15. Total	1,346	1,449	1,809	1,49
Non-financial public in per cent of total	77	74	54	4
Security issues in per cent of GNP	6.2	6.0	6.6	4.

1.   Including a small amount of borrowing by local authorities.
2.   ENEL, ENI, IRI, Autonomous Agency for National Railways, and the Autonomous Agency for National Roads (ANAS).
3.   Including Cassa Depositi e Prestiti.
4.   Including acquisition by foreigners.
Source: OECD, *Financial Statistics.*

1964	1965	1966	1967	1968	1969	1970	1971
207	416	1,232	846	1,052	1,339	1,127	1,773
494	921	670	614	841	778	251	1,037
721	647	861	987	1,189	1,284	1,484	2,229
28	−12	3	−38	−34	−60	−52	−37
12	13	81	21	44	9	5	38
,462	1,985	2,847	2,430	3,092	3,350	2,815	5,040
22	33	83	78	57	117	165	..
531	329	314	261	356	470	768	..
28	44	74	57	60	94	78	..
581	406	471	396	473	681	1,011	972
2,043	2,391	3,318	2,826	3,565	4,031	3,826	6,012
28	17	14	14	13	17	26	16
196	50	227	178	221	1,223	1,304	925
452	1,132	1,322	1,005	1,532	1,146	807	2,329
536	83	64	73	146	55	72	110
859	1,116	1,705	1,570	1,666	1,607	1,643	2,648
2,043	2,391	3,318	2,826	3,565	4,031	3,826	6,012
42	47	51	56	47	40	43	44
6.0	6.5	8.3	6.5	7.6	7.9	6.8	8 0

TABLE A6. CONSUMPTION AND INVESTMENT[1]

BILLION OF LIRE AT 1963 PRICES, SEASONALLY ADJUSTED

		Private consumption plus changes in inventories	Investment in plants, machinery and equipment	Investment in construction sector
1960	I	4,081	506	795
	II	3,967	552	818
	III	4,193	594	835
	IV	4,220	594	832
1961	I	4,213	634	858
	II	4,423	656	850
	III	4,371	675	904
	IV	4,552	682	926
1962	I	4,573	703	949
	II	4,673	700	979
	III	4,758	720	990
	IV	4,754	749	1,017
1963	I	4,926	763	1,008
	II	5,192	809	1,028
	III	5,229	807	1,062
	IV	5,159	803	1,080
1964	I	5,328	776	1,091
	II	5,250	670	1,081
	III	5,039	607	1,052
	IV	5,059	591	1,024
1965	I	5,126	544	1,012
	II	5,258	546	1,013
	III	5,293	572	1,016
	IV	5,525	570	1,023
1966	I	5,568	583	1,031
	II	5,460	579	1,018
	III	5,760	634	1,022
	IV	5,894	667	1,017
1967	I	5,937	705	1,039
	II	5,908	731	1,082
	III	6,097	730	1,134
	IV	6,384	741	1,158
1968	I	6,090	762	1,154
	II	6,198	782	1,166
	III	6,366	818	1,170
	IV	6,413	843	1,332
1969	I	6,538	841	1,366
	II	6,698	914	1,315
	III	6,936	872	1,288
	IV	6,654	769	1,305
1970	I	7,388	920	1,373
	II	7,409	956	1,293
	III	7,360	959	1,232
	IV	7,319	1,001	1,262
1971	I	n.a.	980	1,194
	II	n.a.	947	1,178
	III	n.a.	907	1,175
	IV	n.a.	947	1,200

1. Estimates of quarterly national accounts from ISCO; data used in Bologna econometric model.

OECD SALES AGENTS
DEPOSITAIRES DES PUBLICATIONS DE L'OCDE

ARGENTINE
Libreria de las Naciones
Alsina 500, BUENOS AIRES.

AUSTRALIA – AUSTRALIE
B.C.N. Agencies Pty, Ltd.,
178 Collins Street, MELBOURNE 3000.

AUSTRIA – AUTRICHE
Gerold and Co., Graben 31, WIEN 1.
Sub-Agent: GRAZ: Buchhandlung Jos. A. Kienreich, Sackstrasse 6.

BELGIUM – BELGIQUE
Librairie des Sciences
Coudenberg 76-78 et rue des Eperonniers 56,
B 1000 BRUXELLES 1.

BRAZIL – BRESIL
Mestre Jou S.A., Rua Guaipá 518,
Caixa Postal 24090, 05000 SAO PAULO 10.
Rua Senador Dantas 19 s/205-6, RIO DE
JANEIRO GB.

CANADA
Information Canada
OTTAWA.

DENMARK – DANEMARK
Munksgaard International Booksellers
Nörregade 6, DK-1165 COPENHAGEN K

FINLAND – FINLANDE
Akateeminen Kirjakauppa, Keskuskatu 2,
HELSINKI.

FORMOSA – FORMOSE
Books and Scientific Supplies Services, Ltd.
P.O.B. 83, TAIPEI,
TAIWAN.

FRANCE
Bureau des Publications de l'OCDE
2 rue André-Pascal, 75775 PARIS CEDEX 16
Principaux sous dépositaires :
PARIS : Presses Universitaires de France,
49 bd Saint-Michel, 75005 Paris.
Sciences Politiques (Lib.)
30 rue Saint-Guillaume, 75007 Paris.
13100 AIX-EN-PROVENCE : Librairie de l'Université.
38000 GRENOBLE : Arthaud.
67000 STRASBOURG : Berger-Levrault.
31000 TOULOUSE : Privat.

GERMANY – ALLEMAGNE
Deutscher Bundes-Verlag G.m.b.H.
Postfach 9380, 53 BONN.
Sub-Agents: BERLIN 62: Elwert & Meurer.
HAMBURG: Reuter-Klöckner; und in den
massgebenden Buchhandlungen Deutschlands.

GREECE – GRECE
Librairie Kauffmann, 28 rue du Stade,
ATHENES 132.
Librairie Internationale Jean Mihalopoulos et Fils
75 rue Hermou, B.P. 73, THESSALONIKI.

ICELAND – ISLANDE
Snæbjörn Jónsson and Co., h.f., Hafnarstræti 9,
P.O.B. 1131, REYKJAVIK.

INDIA – INDE
Oxford Book and Stationery Co.:
NEW DELHI, Scindia House.
CALCUTTA, 17 Park Street.

IRELAND – IRLANDE
Eason and Son, 40 Lower O'Connell Street,
P.O.B. 42, DUBLIN 1.

ISRAEL
Emanuel Brown :
9, Shlomzion Hamalka Street, JERUSALEM.
35 Allenby Road, and 48 Nahlath Benjamin St.,
TEL-AVIV.

ITALY – ITALIE
Libreria Commissionaria Sansoni :
Via Lamarmora 45, 50121 FIRENZE.
Via Bartolini 29, 20155 MILANO.
sous-dépositaires :
Editrice e Libreria Herder,
Piazza Montecitorio 120, 00186 ROMA.
Libreria Hoepli, Via Hoepli 5, 20121 MILANO.
Libreria Lattes, Via Garibaldi 3, 10122 TORINO.
La diffusione delle edizioni OCDE è inoltre assicurata dalle migliori librerie nelle città più importanti.

JAPAN – JAPON
Maruzen Company Ltd.,
6 Tori-Nichome Nihonbashi, TOKYO 103,
P.O.B. 5050, Tokyo International 100-31.

LEBANON – LIBAN
Redico
Immeuble Edison, Rue Bliss, B.P. 5641
BEYROUTH.

THE NETHERLANDS – PAYS-BAS
W.P. Van Stockum
Buitenhof 36, DEN HAAG.

NEW ZEALAND – NOUVELLE-ZELANDE
Government Printing Office,
Mulgrave Street (Private Bag), WELLINGTON
and Government Bookshops at
AUCKLAND (P.O.B. 5344)
CHRISTCHURCH (P.O.B. 1721)
HAMILTON (P.O.B. 857)
DUNEDIN (P.O.B. 1104).

NORWAY – NORVEGE
Johan Grundt Tanums Bokhandel,
Karl Johansgate 41/43, OSLO 1.

PAKISTAN
Mirza Book Agency, 65 Shahrah Quaid-E-Azam,
LAHORE 3.

PORTUGAL
Livraria Portugal, Rua do Carmo 70, LISBOA.

SPAIN – ESPAGNE
Mundi Prensa, Castelló 37, MADRID 1.
Libreria Bastinos de José Bosch, Pelayo 52,
BARCELONA 1.

SWEDEN – SUEDE
Fritzes, Kungl. Hovbokhandel,
Fredsgatan 2, 11152 STOCKHOLM 16.

SWITZERLAND – SUISSE
Librairie Payot, 6 rue Grenus, 1211 GENEVE 11
et à LAUSANNE, NEUCHATEL, VEVEY,
MONTREUX, BERNE, BALE, ZURICH.

TURKEY – TURQUIE
Librairie Hachette, 469 Istiklal Caddesi, Beyoglu,
ISTANBUL et 12 Ziya Gökalp Caddesi, ANKARA.

UNITED KINGDOM – ROYAUME-UNI
H.M. Stationery Office, P.O.B. 569, LONDON
SE1 9NH
or
49 High Holborn
LONDON WC1V 6HB (personal callers)
Branches at: EDINBURGH, BIRMINGHAM,
BRISTOL, MANCHESTER, CARDIFF,
BELFAST.

UNITED STATES OF AMERICA
OECD Publications Center, Suite 1207,
1750 Pennsylvania Ave, N.W.
WASHINGTON, D.C. 20006. Tel.: (202)298-8755.

VENEZUELA
Libreria del Este, Avda. F. Miranda 52,
Edificio Galipan, CARACAS.

YUGOSLAVIA – YOUGOSLAVIE
Jugoslovenska Knjiga, Terazije 27, P.O.B. 36,
BEOGRAD.

Les commandes provenant de pays où l'OCDE n'a pas encore désigné de dépositaire
peuvent être adressées à :
OCDE, Bureau des Publications, 2 rue André-Pascal, 75775 Paris CEDEX 16
Orders and inquiries from countries where sales agents have not yet been appointed may be sent to
OECD, Publications Office, 2 rue André-Pascal, 75775 Paris CEDEX 16

OECD   PUBLICATIONS
2, rue André-Pascal
75775 PARIS CEDEX 16
No. 31,685.   1973.

●

PRINTED IN FRANCE